THE SEVENTEEN MILLION

THE MACMILLAN COMPANY
NEW YORK · BOSTON · CHICAGO · DALLAS
ATLANTA · SAN FRANCISCO

MACMILLAN & CO., LIMITED
LONDON · BOMBAY · CALCUTTA
MELBOURNE

THE MACMILLAN COMPANY
OF CANADA, LIMITED
TORONTO

THE
SEVENTEEN
MILLION

BY

OGDEN L. MILLS

NEW YORK

THE MACMILLAN COMPANY

1937

PRINTED IN THE UNITED STATES OF AMERICA
BY THE STRATFORD PRESS, INC., NEW YORK

CONTENTS

THE SEVENTEEN MILLION

CHAPTER I

INDIVIDUALISM OR COLLECTIVISM?

In November, 1936, some seventeen million voters recorded their opposition to the direction in which we are now traveling. Though a minority, they constitute a large percentage of the total electorate. If they hold together, these seventeen million can profoundly influence both public opinion and public policy. And the day may not be far distant when they may exercise a preponderant influence.

For them to speak with a united voice they must have a common philosophy. For this minority to become the majority they must present a political program based on that philosophy.

This book is an attempt by one of the seventeen million to define the philosophy; and to give the outlines of a program.

However, before discussing the future, it is necessary that we take a look back along the historical road people have traveled, so we may refresh our memories on some essential background.

The world prior to the Great War was a very different one from that of today. The preceding century had witnessed the growth of humanitarianism—the spread of democratic ideals—the development of free enter-

1

prise—the expansion of international trade and of intercourse between nations, until practically the entire globe had become intimately united as an immense cooperative workshop.

It was an age of individualism, not only in the sense that the individual was looked upon as the source of all creative effort and progress, but that full recognition was given to his dignity and rights as a man. Men ceased to be pawns of the State or the mere instruments of dynastic policies and ambitions. They asserted their right to govern themselves, to direct their own destinies, to think, speak and worship as they pleased, to be free from tyranny, to live in peace, to trade with each other across national boundaries, and to enjoy the opportunity of earning their living under decent conditions. Men of more than ordinary ability and force of will were given opportunity for creative effort, by which they themselves, and many others because of them, made very rapid progress. Opportunity was theirs, not only because new frontiers were opened in land and in the applied sciences, but because their potentialities were recognized and respected.

The spirit of the age found expression in democracy in government; dignity, freedom and responsibility in the life of the individual; free competitive enterprise in economics; and peace and commerce among the nations.

That the expressed ideals were not fully realized is certainly true. Some interpreted freedom as a license to bargain unjustly for the services of their fellows, and forced contractual relations on employees that certainly were not free from the standpoint of the employee. There was a vast amount of inequality, poverty and injustice. Men continued to prey on their fellows. The up and down swings of economic cycles marred the symmetry of a steadily rising curve.

Feudalism persisted in certain great countries. There were diversities of interests among the nations. Racial antagonisms still divided them. And under autocratic and unwise leaders these influences resulted in the universal disaster of the World War.

But, in spite of all this, that pre-war century was one of greater peace, greater abundance and greater progress in terms of the well-being of the average man and woman than the world had ever known.

If we consider the state of Europe in the second half of the eighteenth century, we find a population of about 170,000,000 people, the overwhelming majority of whom lived on a bare subsistence level.

In Germany in 1800 the average income of the Prussian peasant was about twenty dollars a year.

At the end of the seventeenth century one-half of the population of England had an average family income of fifteen pounds a year, or less.

In 1910 we find about 450,000,000 people occupying the same territory and enjoying—outside of Russia—an infinitely higher standard of living. In Great Britain, for illustration, the level of real incomes in the years before the World War was four times as great as during the Napoleonic period.

What had happened during the comparatively short period of 100 years to bring about this progress—to enable the same territory to support almost three times as many people on the basis of a very much higher standard of living?

The coming of the machine age and the technological development? It seems to me we must go deeper than machine or technological development.

Please remember that a Roman of the time of Augustus would have found little to surprise him had he been suddenly transported to the England of the eighteenth century—that is, excepting for gunpowder and printing. He would have been familiar with the great buildings, the fine roads, the means of transportation by land and water, agricultural processes and the different handicrafts. For him, the world, to practically all intents and purposes, would have been standing still for 1,800 years. One hundred years later this same Roman would have been stupefied.

What had happened? Certainly man's mind and imagination had not improved, as witness the comparative state of the arts. His nature and character had not been transformed. What, then, had loosed his creative genius? Why had his inventive genius so suddenly come to life with such vigor?

I can give you the answer in one word—freedom!

In 1776 two events of transcendant importance occurred. They were the American Declaration of Independence, and the publication of Adam Smith's "Wealth of Nations."

The American Revolution and the adoption of a Constitution which guaranteed the individual from the tyranny of government had worldwide effect. With the coming of the French Revolution and, paradoxical as it may be, the onsweep of the French National Armies, the spirit of liberty extinguished the old order. The planned and controlled economies were thrown into political ash cans. Within three-quarters of a century political freedom had been won in most countries, and economic freedom everywhere save in such nations as Russia.

After eighteen centuries of stagnation, the world literally bounded forward—with mankind enjoying greater general well-being than at any time in all history.

According to Sir George Paish, "in the century up to the war, the world's income expanded five-fold after having taken all the other centuries to grow up to a very small figure, and that was principally due to the fact that international trade expanded no less than twelve-fold."

That all progress is born of individual effort and that man's creative genius flourishes only in an atmosphere of freedom had been proved beyond question. How otherwise can you account for the fact that when technological improvements came with giant strides they originated for the most part in those countries where the individual enjoyed the greatest freedom—the United States and England? From Russia and Spain came nothing.

Then came the World War, with its frightful slaughter, its immense destruction of wealth, its unnatural expansion and diversion of productive energy, its hammer-blow to the intricate and delicate mechanism of trade, commerce and the monetary systems, and the complete centralization of all power in the hands of governments.

When the guns were silenced, men and women turned hopefully to the task of restoring their shattered dwelling in the light of their ancient faith. But the dislocations, the new strains and stresses, and the fatal weaknesses engendered by the war were too great. The new and flimsy edifices they erected collapsed under the impact of the Great Depression.

Despairing people turned away from the individual and his freedom to discover new gods . . . and, in so doing, only disinterred ancient idols.

Today, everywhere, individual liberties are being curtailed and destroyed. Democracy and self-government are scrapped. Individuals are once more the pawns of arbitrary rulers whose policies are determined by nationalistic aims, with war as their ultimate and supreme weapon. Greater and greater rigidities undermine the flexibility and adaptiveness of economic systems. Planned and controlled economies emerge. "Tariffs, exchange restrictions, quotas, import prohibitions, barter trade agreements, central trade clearing arrangements —all the fusty relics of mediaeval trade regulations, discredited through five hundred years of theory and hard experience, are dragged out." The doctrines of self-containment and self-sufficiency reenforce the rigidities and restrictions of planning, and give rise to new international antagonisms.

Nations are feverishly rearming. New instruments of destruction are being forged from diminishing resources. People whose salvation depends upon mutual cooperation in the peaceful process of reconstruction are staring at each other with growing mistrust and antagonism. International trade languishes. Standards of living are falling. Great nations are being threatened with economic collapse—and, to sustain economic life, governments are creating purchasing power by exhausting a rapidly vanishing credit.

Or, to put it quickly:

Today, the world seems to be driven by an irresistible fate to an irretrievable disaster.

It is not a heartening picture I have drawn for you —but, it is a true one.

It is with that picture in mind that, at the outset, I want to ask certain questions—questions, the answers to which are at the core of my political philosophy:

1. In the long run will not men and women, through democratic process, govern themselves more wisely and beneficially than any dictator?

2. Is the abundance so essential to a higher standard of living more likely to be generated by the creative energy of the individual operating in a system of free enterprise than by the sterile direction of a government bureaucracy?

3. Is the peace we long for more likely to find a secure foundation in economic cooperation among peoples rather than in narrow nationalism?

4. Are those spiritual values which are directly related to individual liberty—freedom of religion, of thought, of speech, of education, and of science—worth preserving?

If these questions are answered in the affirmative— as I believe they must be—then somewhere men and women must once again go forth in battle for a great cause.

That is the task I would assign to the seventeen million and to a revitalized Republican Party.

To those who think of the Republican Party as the party of reaction, of big business, and of high protection, such a notion may sound completely fantastic or completely insincere.

Yet I would remind you that the Republican Party was born of a great liberal movement in behalf of human freedom; that for over half a century, with only two brief intermissions, it governed the nation throughout a period of unparalleled social and economic progress; and that, in spite of twenty-five years of apparent disintegration, through a strange combination of circumstances it is today the sole residuary legatee of the tradition in the United States, that the individual man has rights independent of and prior in nature to government, and that no government may deny him these rights without arresting progress and making men slaves.

The division in the ranks of the Republican Party which definitely appeared in 1910 and culminated in the third party movement in 1912 was never healed. From that day on, the Party lacked national unity and cohesion. It lost its sense of direction.

The unity achieved in 1918 and 1920 was not deep. Victory in 1920 was due more to anti-war, anti-European and anti-Wilson feeling than it was to Republican cohesion and strength. The steady waning of the party's influence over the course of the next ten years in such key states as New York makes this clear.

It won in 1924 because times were better and because of confidence in Coolidge. It won again in 1928 because of boom prosperity and confidence in Hoover. Neither election indicated that the people had any great interest in the Republican Party or the Democratic Party, as such.

The truth is that the old issues upon which the parties divided had largely disappeared. There were no fundamental differences between them. Even in the matter of the tariff the Democrats, for the most part, had become protectionists in practice if not in theory. Although the world was confronted with new conditions and novel problems from which new issues were converging, in the twelve years, which came to an end in 1932, these issues had not emerged in the United States.

This is not to be wondered at since our efforts from 1920 to 1929 were directed largely in trying to restore the pre-war world we had known. In other words, it was a period of reconstruction—reconstruction which at one time appeared to have been achieved.

At home the energies of the Government were directed toward demobilizing the war machine, restoring peace-time conditions, putting the Government's house in order, reducing the burden of taxes, and laying the foundations of renewed prosperity. Industrial progress was achieved on a large scale, although agricultural recovery lagged stubbornly; and in time unhealthy speculative activities brought inevitable retribution.

Abroad, Europe sought to find peace through a new system of collective security. Our contributions to the cause of peace were the Washington Disarmament Conference, the Seven Power Pact, and later the Kellogg-Briand Pact. One by one budgets were balanced. Currencies were restored to some kind of stability. The gold standard was reinstated. Central banks cooperated. Intergovernmental debts were settled on some sort of basis. Trade restrictions were relaxed—although they were immediately replaced by excessively high tariffs.

Some semblance of economic order appeared in the world. Trade revived and production increased enormously. International investment was resumed on an unprecedented scale. The value of stocks and other securities rose.

But side by side with these evidences of world recovery there were deep-seated maladjustments. The universal dislocations had not been mended. The social, political, and economic forces engendered by a disastrous war and an equally disastrous peace had not spent their force. They culminated in the Great Depression.

Post-war reconstruction had failed. The task was more formidable than anyone had dreamed. We are still wrestling with it.

The history of the Hoover Administration is the history of a series of courageous—and with one or two notable exceptions—constructive and successful measures intended to parry one devastating blow after another. Considering the fact that we were in the downward spiral of an immense deflation, these measures were necessarily defensive in character, and intended to prevent disintegration until the normal forces of recovery could assert themselves.

It is sometimes said that these measures invoked the power of the Federal Government on such a comprehensive scale that Mr. Hoover laid the foundation for the New Deal.

Excepting in the case of the Agricultural Marketing Act, and of the Farm Board, I cannot agree to the validity of this charge. There is a great distinction between government leadership and government coercion. Likewise, there is a great distinction between support by government and supplanting by government. And, in addition, there is all the difference in the world between a spirit and a purpose determined to preserve existing institutions and one equally determined to weaken or pervert them.

While, from a strict viewpoint, the Hoover program may have represented an innovation; and, under the stress of a great emergency, a temporary departure from traditional practices, it did no violence to basic principles.

This, Mr. Hoover made abundantly clear in his 1932 speech of acceptance, when he said:

The function of the Federal Government in these times is to use its reserve powers and its strength for the protection of citizens and local governments by support to our institutions against forces beyond their control. It is not the function of the Government to relieve individuals of their responsibilities to their neighbors, or to relieve private institutions of their responsibilities to the public, or of local governments to the states, or of state governments to the Federal Government. In giving that protection and that aid the Federal Government must insist that all of them exert their responsibilities in full. It is vital that the programs of the Government shall not compete with or replace any of them but shall add to their initiative and their strength. It is vital that by the use of public revenues and public credit in emergency the Nation shall be strengthened and not weakened.

The solution of our many problems which arise from the shifting scene of national life is not to be found in haphazard experimentation or by revolution. It must be through organic development of our national life under these ideals. It must secure that cooperative action which builds initiative and strength outside of government. It does not follow, because our difficulties are stupendous, because there are some souls timorous enough to doubt the validity and effectiveness of our ideals and our system, that we must turn to a State controlled, or State directed social or economic system to cure our troubles. That is not liberalism; it is tyranny. It is the regimentation of men under autocratic bureaucracy with all its extinction of liberty, of hope and of opportunity. Of course, no man of understanding says that our system works perfectly. It does not. The human race is not perfect. Nevertheless, the movement of a true civilization is toward freedom rather than regimentation. This is our ideal.

Thus we have held that the Federal Government should in the presence of great national danger use its powers to give leadership to the initiative, the courage, and the fortitude of the people themselves; but it must insist upon individual, community and state responsibility. That it should furnish leadership to assure the coordination and unity of all existing agencies, governmental and private, for economic and humanitarian action. That where it becomes necessary to meet emergencies beyond the power of these agencies by the creation of new Government instrumentalities, they should be of such character as not to supplant, or weaken, but rather to supplement and strengthen, the initiative and enterprise of the people. That they must, directly or indirectly, serve all the people. Above all, that they should be set up in such form that once the emergency is passed they can and must be demobilized and withdrawn, leaving our governmental, economic and social structure strong and whole.

In the campaign of 1932 the Democrats adopted as their platform an admirable restatement of their historic position. The Republicans stood on the record of the Hoover administration.

Mr. Roosevelt accepted his party's platform without qualification. He went through the entire campaign without giving a hint of how completely he intended to jettison it. Mr. Hoover sensed what was coming. He repeatedly challenged Mr. Roosevelt to be frank, but without success.

The people, wearied by the long depression and determined to have a change, turned a deaf ear. Except for the obvious fact that Mr. Hoover was going out and Mr. Roosevelt was coming in, there was an air of unreality about it all.

But there has been nothing unreal about events since.

We have seen the government undertake to control production in agriculture, manufacturing and mining. We have seen it attempt the regulation of prices, wages and conditions of labor. We have seen it determine the volume and flow of credit. We have seen the arbitrary debasement of our currency. We have seen the Federal Government enter the field of private enterprise in competition with its own citizens. We have seen a whole body of new legislation intended to establish a planned economy.

And, having seen all that, we do not need the President's declaration that he has created "new instruments of public power"—that the Federal Government is responsible for the solution of the problems of the individual—to know that we are face to face with a new philosophy; or that a new political party has been born.

What is equally important is that, for the time being, the American people have accepted this new political philosophy; and have charged the National Government with full responsibility for the economic conditions under which they live and work.

For want of a better name we may call this new party the New Deal Party. While it has taken over the name and organization of the historic Democratic Party, it has nothing in common with it. In fact—and as every Democrat knows—it repudiates every major article of the Democratic faith.

That is why I say the Democratic Party, as it has been known, has ceased to exist.

This is almost as true of the Republican Party. The issues which gave it vigor in its prime have vanished. The conditions which ensured its political supremacy have disappeared. Pennsylvania, Michigan and Ohio are doubtful states. New York, Illinois and Massachusetts have already gone over to the other side.

Today there exists a strongly organized, well-led militant New Deal Party—and, I might add, it is a well-fed New Deal Party, as well. It proclaims a political philosophy new to America.

On the other hand, there are some 17,000,000 quite thoroughly disorganized individuals who vote as Republicans; and who, as I have said, are the heirs of the American tradition, there being no other claimants.

Today, two major political forces are fighting for supremacy in the world.

One is the all-powerful Collectivism.

The other is Individualism.

I believe the hope of mankind is in free individuals determined to keep what is worth preserving, especially their freedom to choose.

But if in this country the seventeen million who voted "no" are to be united in a revitalized and militant organization, they must have leadership. They must have the capacity to develop a program. They must demonstrate that they are not fighting for empty and outworn ideals. They must prove that they can deal realistically with the problems of the day. They must be prepared to satisfy the legitimate demands of the people. Above all, they must have unshakable faith and unchallengeable sincerity.

In view of the present-day perversion of the meaning of the term "liberal," I would make this the party of conservatism.

Conservatism in this sense. That in a world which seeks progress through the repudiation of accepted truths and the destruction of established institutions, good and bad alike, we mean to conserve the foundations of American life. We mean to hold to the principles born of the accumulated experience of our race. We believe that they are as valid today as yesterday; and that they are fully capable of adaptation to the new problems of a new world.

That a conservative party, fully alive to the needs of the day, but with its roots grounded in the American tradition, can soon become the dominant party, I entertain no doubt. Americans do not favor the destruction of their institutions. Once alive to where the present movement leads them, they will assert their will in no uncertain way.

Even on the basis of the Roosevelt landslide, it would take only a twelve per cent shift in votes to give the opposition a majority—and there are millions who voted for Mr. Roosevelt because of recovery and their faith in him who have no intention to become the subjects of a collectivist state.

The American people of today have no intention of bestowing on the State that divine right of absolutism their forefathers took away from kings so long ago.

CHAPTER II

THE COLLECTIVIST STATE

THE New Movement had its immediate origin in the disorder, distress and despair left in the wake of the greatest war in history. The war wrecked the economic organism of the world, and inflicted immeasurable distress on countless individuals.

It did more. It bred a spirit of violence and of disrespect for established institutions. It destroyed the faith, the optimism, and the idealism that had inspired the world for a century or more.

The basic political and economic philosophy of the New Movement, however, existed long before the war. It is directly derived from the teachings of pre-war Socialists, Communists and Syndicalist writers. It is no accident that both Hitler and Mussolini are ex-Socialists.

In Continental Europe the seeds of distrust in democracy and in representative institutions had long since been sown among all classes of society. The intellectual foundation for a new social order had been laid. As a result, once the impact of the war and the depression had undermined faith in democratic institutions, the transition was effected with extraordinary ease.

Excepting in Russia, and now in Spain, revolutions were accompanied by little or no violence or loss of life. Despairing of their ability to achieve their own salvation, and under the dominating leadership of prophets seeking personal power, the people surrendered control of their destiny to the State without a struggle.

While the Collectivist State assumes different forms in different countries, it has certain common features. It exalts the sovereignty of the State and denies the sovereignty of the people. It rejects as cumbersome and ineffective the machinery of democracy. It scorns personal liberty and personal rights. It denies the ability of the individual to make headway in a modern world. It looks to government as the source of progress rather than to the individual human spirit. For free enterprise, it substitutes planning and control by a centralized bureaucracy. It invokes and inspires an intense spirit of nationalism.

In these respects there is no difference between Fascism and Communism.

They have another feature in common. In theory they rely on the dictatorship of a party—a party which in no sense resembles our political parties, but more closely approximate a military order. The party serves as an instrument of government and, also, as a means of assuring continuity to the regime.

Whatever the theory may be, in practice both Fascism and Communism result in dictatorship by an individual. As the uncontrolled boss of the party he becomes the uncontrolled boss of the country. Which means it elevates one man to supreme authority—one who is no better than the rest of the people, but, by having no reins to check him, is very apt to be worse.

The chief difference between Communism and Fascism is that Communism undertakes the complete liquidation of the existing social and economic order; Fascism, though maintaining outward forms, absorbs the social and economic order into the Corporate State.

The central thought in both is that by acting collectively, men can eliminate inequality and injustice; increase the general well-being and attain both individual security and general economic stability. It is contended that by bringing all economic forces and elements under the control of government, a more just distribution of the national income can be assured— and that booms and depressions can be ironed out.

Three general criticisms of the collectivist philosophy can be made.

1. It disregards the nature of man.
2. It has never honestly faced the problem of planning where abundance exists.
3. It is autocracy and tyranny in government.

Man, as an individual, is the most supremely important fact in our universe. Men collectively have purpose, direction and creative ability only in so far as they are furnished by individuals. It is true man is a creature of material wants, desires and ambitions, but he is also a spiritual being. And, whether in the world of matter in the satisfaction of material wants, or in the world of the spirit in his search for truth, he is the only source of creative effort.

Deprive him of his freedom, imprison his spirit

within the narrow confines of arbitrary authority, and his creative faculties soon grow sterile.

Therefore, any philosophy whose sole concern is for mankind collectively, which glorifies mass mediocrity at the cost of individual genius, which is careless of spiritual values, and which ignores the conditions essential to creative effort, is a false doctrine.

It is a philosophy which directly denies the principles upon which our country was founded. The first and foremost of these is that the individual is supreme; that man is endowed, not by government but by his Creator, with certain unalienable rights; that to preserve these rights governments are instituted; and that governments derive their powers only from the consent of the governed.

In other words, man is regarded as "a free moral personality, the creature of God, and the maker of his own destiny."

Contrast this with a doctrine which holds that the citizen has no rights save those allowed him by another man in the name of the State, which suppresses individuality, and whose god, in Russia at least, is uniformity,—uniformity of thought, of life and of reward.

To them the individual is of no consequence. Liberties acquired through centuries of struggle are suppressed. Freedom of thought, of speech, of religion, of education and of science disappear. Men live in a spiritual vacuum, though we do find a mystical veneration of nationalism and racialism in the Fascist States, and Communism does seem to develop an almost religious fervor.

"Fascism," says Mussolini, "accepts the individual only in so far as his interests coincide with those of the State * * *. All in the State, nothing outside of the State, nothing against the State."

Neither in Germany, Russia nor Italy is independence of thought tolerated. Any dissent from the prevailing dogma is ruthlessly suppressed. Concentration camps, blood purges and mass executions, supplemented by wholesale propaganda and the control of all sources of information and of education, are expected to produce the desired conformity.

As Mr. Walter Lippmann has said:

It is one of the most curious experiments ever undertaken; this attempt, in an age when the means of communication have been stupendously magnified, to control by government bureaus all the organs of intelligence in order to remake man, character, faith. The German experiment, except to those who are its victims, is particularly interesting and, like the offer of a strong man to let himself be vivisected, a great contribution to political science. For the Germans are the most gifted and most highly educated people who ever devoted the full strength of a modern state to stopping the exchange of ideas; they are the most highly organized nation which ever devoted all the coercive power of government to the abolition of the intellectual life of its people; they are the most learned people who ever pretended to believe that the premises and the conclusion of all inquiry may be fixed by political fiat.

But it is not only in its denial of conditions favorable to human development and progress that the new movement errs. It has never honestly faced the technical difficulties of planning.

As two British economists have well stated:

Whatever the motive for planning, two preliminary comments may be made. First, no country yet possesses the capacity for government or for collective management, nor yet the detailed statistical information, to justify an experiment in wholesale planning even if this were in other respects desirable, which is by no means proved. Secondly, no theory has yet produced a better mechanism for satisfying wants than the combination of individual enterprise in production with the price mechanism in distribution.

There have been many planned economies in the world. Without exception, they were scarcity systems. Not one ever succeeded in banishing even famine, much less poverty.

What is equally significant is that planning is completely helpless when confronted with abundance.

By abundance I mean, for the purpose of present discussion, a family income not only adequate for necessities but with a surplus available for spending on the basis of preference rather than of necessity.

In the United States in normal times, while there are altogether too many families whose incomes are wholly devoted to sheer necessities, there are many millions more whose choice in spending extends over an almost unlimited list of articles of every kind. And this goes on year after year, in good times and in bad. As a matter of fact, even in the depression years the living standard of the great majority of our people was higher than the prosperous standard of practically every nation.

The picture of millions of men and women, each primarily concerned with his, or her, own interests, working for one another, producing goods and services for one another, and producing them in such kinds and quantities as to satisfy both available income and extraordinarily varied demand, is an amazing spectacle.

Yet, that is precisely what occurs in a properly functioning and well-balanced free competitive economy. That such an economy does not always function smoothly, we know. But that it can so function is attested by the fact that only a few years ago scarcely anyone knew that a problem existed.

The key to the mystery is the price mechanism. Market prices, worked out competitively, tell people the things to do that other people want done.

And, note this well:

In any economy of abundance the ultimate causation rests on the demand side of the price mechanism rather than on the production side.

This is the insurmountable obstacle to planning.

Though the system appears to be chaotic and planless, such is not the case. Its manifold activities result from the individual plans of many intelligent, trained and experienced men and women who do not make haphazard guesses. They make their calculations on the basis of well-established factors and rules.

Costs are nothing more than other prices. So, on the production side, price in relation to costs determines what goods will be produced and in what quantities. If prices are unreasonably high above costs in any given line, it indicates that here is an unsatisfied consumer demand. Consequently, capital flows in that direction, thus increasing employment and production. Conversely, when prices are so low in relation to costs as to threaten the profit margin, labor and capital move in other directions.

On the distribution side a flexible price mechanism is equally effective. When the prices of goods rise, consumption tends to fall; just as when prices fall consumption increases. Since at the same time production tends to increase in the first case, and to decline in the second, the shortage, or over-supply—as the case may be—in any given commodity is thus corrected. Where prices, labor and capital are free, these forces exert a constant pull in the direction of a balanced supply and demand, and of the production of goods in the right proportions.

If the economic machine were not so immense, and the human mind had the capacity to grasp it in its entirety, it would see that here is no planless chaos. Actually what the eye would see would be a highly integrated mechanism responding to the multiplicity of plans which, though seemingly unrelated, cause it to function with a high degree of efficiency.

Dr. Benjamin Anderson, Jr., pointed this out, by saying:

Economic life, as we have known it, has been, in large measure, an unconscious thing in the sense that no mind or no group of minds has seen the whole picture, and certainly no one mind or group of minds has directed the whole picture. Intelligence runs through it, but it is the intelligence of individuals or organizations seeking their own particular wages or their own particular profits, seeing their own sources of supply, seeing their own markets, but not seeing with any great clearness the movements of the system as a whole. * * *

Here, then, is the central contrast between our present system and a planned economy—in the problem of coordi-, nating the economic activities of men and making a social order. Our present system relies upon the unconscious, automatic functioning of the markets. A "controlled economy" must do it, if at all, by conscious public planning, a central brain guiding, controlling and regimenting the masses of men, controlling production, controlling consumption, controlling the distribution of wealth and, in a large measure, regulating the lives and activities of men.

To develop a planned economy, it is apparent that people must have at least some sign-posts by which to guide their efforts. These they have not got.

Having eliminated the competitive processes and the price mechanism through which free enterprise functions, the planners are left without guide or standard by which to determine what goods are to be produced, how the relationship between different lines of production are to be established and coordinated, and how consumers' choices can be expressed. Of course, they may arbitrarily determine what people ought to have. But they have no means of knowing what the people may want to have at a given price. In a country where people are free to spend their income as they please, it is impossible to plan a production program.

The planners have been misled by governmental control of production under war conditions. Under such circumstances, the government feels free to ration all consumers—remember the meatless days during the war?—and, for the most part, the people are quite ready to comply. This done, the productive energies of the nation can be canalized so as to meet specific needs as outlined by the General Staff. This can be done because there is a definite objective.

This also is true of a country such as Russia, where the real problem is one of supplying the people with the bare necessities of life. Here, again, the objective of directing the productive facilities is to provide necessities. In a lesser degree this also is true of Germany and Italy, for they can hardly be said to enjoy anything faintly resembling abundance. And, in addition, in all three of these countries there is the extra factor that their economies are directed to the ultimate objective of war.

In other words, each has a definite, if two-fold, objective: One, so to manage the productive machinery as to satisfy the basic needs of the people; and, two, to put the nation on a war-time basis in time of peace.

These conditions are not present here. Our national income is not only sufficient to provide necessities, but a great number of comforts and luxuries for the majority of the people. Nor have our people any thought of being put on a war-time basis.

So the planners in this country—and, as you know, we have them in Washington—have no criterion by which to determine the volume and kind of production necessary to meet a demand which is constantly shifting. For not only are tastes susceptible to rapid changes, but their satisfaction is influenced by prices. Correctly to estimate demand, not only must the planners determine future tastes in advance, but they must also be able to foresee proper price relationships of hundreds of thousands of articles, ranging from raw materials to semi-finished and finished goods. If demand as influenced by prices has not been accurately gauged from top to bottom of the entire list, there will be a shortage in some directions and a surplus in others. How could the planners explain that?

The plain truth is:

There can be no planned production to meet a free demand!

If we insist on controlling production, we must be prepared to ration consumption.

This means compelling everyone to spend his or her wages—and his or her savings—as directed by a government agency. Which, in turn, means telling the people when to buy, what to buy, and how much. No planner has yet had the fortitude to publicize this requirement.

Nor will they. The fact is, they will not even face this final factor.

Beyond that, a planned economy is the enemy of progress. All the planners—you see, they are human in spite of their aspirations—can possibly know are the conditions prevailing at any given moment. That is why, as contrasted with a free economy which is in a constant state of flux and growth, a planned order tends to be stationary.

For instance, some thirty years ago existing automobile plants were adequate to supply the demand for the few thousand cars that could be sold at the then existing high prices. Could any bureaucracy in Washington, or elsewhere, have foreseen that productive efficiency would so reduce the price of cars as to bring them within the reach of millions of pocketbooks? The answer is, of course not. That fact alone would have tended to freeze the automobile industry at its 1907 stage of development.

It needs no imagination to figure out what that means. In 1907 the production of automobiles was counted in the thousands; today, the annual production figures reach into the millions, which, translated, become wages to countless numbers of people, everywhere.

Finally, a planned economy calls for an all-powerful government; for, if government is to regiment people as producers, and ration them as consumers, it must have complete control over their lives. And this sort of a government calls for something which to all intents and purposes is a permanent administration.

Hitler was voted in by a majority of the German people in an apparently honest election. But just let the German people try to vote him out.

Thus autocracy in government is the inevitable consequence of collectivist planning. Ballots may put the planners in. Only bullets can put them out. Stalin, Hitler and Mussolini are not accidents. Dictatorships are an inescapable element in the new economic order. They are just as essential a part of a collectivist society as democratic institutions are a part of a free society.

I am not suggesting that the establishment of a centralized authoritarian government is being deliberately planned in Washington. But, in examining a philosophy of government, it is legitimate to explore all its complications and consequences. And, once we admit that the Federal Government is responsible for eliminating all inequalities and injustices; for regulating the economic conditions under which the individual citizens work and live; for stabilizing the national economy; and for assuring prosperity and security to all, the very mechanics of the situation will hurry us to extremes much faster than the advocates of the new philosophy being preached here realize.

The danger lies not so much in the overthrow of our historic institutions by direct and violent revolution, although the delegation of legislative powers to the Executive, the destruction of States' rights, and the proposed "packing of the Supreme Court" are all revolutionary acts.

The real danger lies in the loosing of forces and the adoption of practices that will almost imperceptibly destroy the strength of these institutions.

Collectivism and individualism are irreconcilable concepts; and individualism simply cannot survive a continuous process of erosion, any more than a business which is financed out of a private purse can long compete with one financed by the public purse.

Already some of the tendencies and results I have described have begun to appear. We have not gone nearly so far as they have in Europe—but, we are on our way!

On the economic side, let us consider two of the principal New Movement measures, the A.A.A. and the N.R.A.

These measures were intended to bring production in agriculture and in industry under the control of the Federal Government. Both were Fascistic in conception, since control was not direct but was exercised through the medium of monopolistic groups of existing producers.

The Federal Government used its power, its influence, and the people's money to organize the farmers so they could restrict production, raise prices, and thereby deny the consumer the benefit of increased efficiency and compel him to support the inefficient producer.

The N.R.A. was attractively described as self-government in industry. What this meant was control of industry by those engaged in any particular line at that particular moment—efficient and inefficient alike. Newcomers were frozen out. In the name of "stability," introduction of fresh capital was forbidden. By the same token so were any revolutionary changes by way of invention and improved process. Labor was satisfied with increased money wages. Manufacturers, because they could fix prices, were indifferent to increased costs.

The inevitable result of such planning is to restrict production, to diminish national income, to perpetuate inefficiency and to bar progress.

It is obvious that such measures as the N.R.A. and the A.A.A. are not guide-posts along the road to abundance. The important point to note, however, is that this sort of intervention by government destroys the price mechanism and the competitive process—the two most vital elements in the existing economic order.

At the same time, the principles upon which we have built our fabric of government are threatened with destruction.

These principles have their roots deep in history. They represent the accumulated experience of the human race. They define the conditions which, during

the course of a long struggle, men and women have learned are essential for the preservation of freedom.
Allow me to repeat them:

1. Centralization of power leads to despotism. As Thomas Jefferson said, "When all government, domestic and foreign, in little as in great things, shall be drawn to Washington as the center of all power * * * it will become as venal and oppressive as the government from which we separated."

2. Executive, legislative and judicial powers must be sharply separated, "to the end," as declared in the Constitution of Massachusetts, "that ours may be a government of laws and not of men."

3. Individual liberty and the rights of minorities require not only the protection of a Bill of Rights, but of fearless and independent tribunals.

4. Political liberty and economic freedom are inseparable; and when the government controls the citizen's means of livelihood, it controls the citizen.

Accordingly, our ancestors tied into the pattern of our institutions certain essential principles:

(a) A Federal Government with powers limited to those specifically granted.

(b) Distribution of those powers among the three divisions of government.

(c) A broad measure of Home Rule, assured by the provision that all powers not delegated to the Federal Government are reserved to the States, respectively, or to the people.

(d) Individual liberty, guaranteed by the Bill of Rights.

(e) Economic freedom, regulated by law.

(f) Majority rule.

These safeguards have been weakened by the impact of the New Movement.

Unmindful of Jefferson's admonition, there has been an immense concentration of power. Law after law has been enacted giving the government in Washington jurisdiction over matters definitely reserved to the States. True, these laws were declared unconstitutional. But, supposing the Supreme Court is brought under the control of the Executive, then what? Can you believe the Constitution will be a bar to their enactment?

At the same time, the power of the purse has been used to undermine the authority of State and local governments. In four years the Federal Government has spent more than $13,000,000,000 on matters hitherto the duties of State and local governments. Has that been done so the Executive might get direct control over the lives of millions of people far removed from Washington? I merely ask the question, leaving the answer to you.

What of the second great safeguard, the division of powers within the Federal Government?

The record shows that under this Administration the Congress has repeatedly delegated its legislative powers to the Executive. In one case the surrender was so complete that Mr. Justice Cardozo was forced to exclaim: "This is delegation run riot. No such plenitude of power is susceptible of transfer."

Nor was the abdication by Congress an accident. It is a necessity if government is to undertake the control of the economic life of the nation. In defense of the usurpation of these powers, the argument is put forth that legislative processes in a democracy are too slow and cumbersome to deal promptly with the rapidly changing and multitudinous aspects of business policy.

If that is true, then it is equally true that an appeal to the courts is inconsistent with the direct, prompt and efficient action essential to the conduct of business and economic affairs by government. Aside from the necessity of circumventing the Constitution, this is the reason which lies behind the desire of the leaders of the New Movement to curb the independent authority of the judicial branch of the Government.

The destruction of the independence of the courts is dreadful business. The integrity of Constitutional Government is undermined. Civil liberties are threatened with extinction. There is such an immoral aspect to packing a court of justice that both government and law are brought into contempt. The present widespread lawlessness is not unconnected with the continued attacks made upon the Supreme Court by those in high positions.

In wiping out the division of powers within the government, the second great safeguard against arbitrary authority and personal government disappears. Do we want more personal government? There are plenty of examples of it in the world today. Take a look at them and make up your minds.

Next we come to free enterprise. That one of the cardinal principles of the New Deal is to suppress free enterprise cannot be denied. There is no disputing the fact that free government and free enterprise go hand in hand. Political liberty does not long survive the loss of economic freedom.

With States' rights ignored, with the Federal Government becoming one of unlimited rather than limited authority, with the destruction of the division of powers within the government, with the loss of independence by the courts, and with the threat to economic freedom, our government takes on more and more the appearance of an elective despotism rather than that of our American representative democracy.

Said Jefferson: "An elective despotism was not the government we fought for."

Already one observer, not unfriendly to the President, has remarked that under the present Administration we may have a government for the people, but we no longer have government of the people, and by the people.

When government is no longer one of the people, and by the people, it is simply a question of time before it ceases to be government for the people.

But it is said we still have majority rule, and free elections continue to assure popular control. How long can elections remain free after government attains power over the lives of men and women? Today, in Germany, we hear Hitler boasting that he is speaking for the German people—because they gave him a mandate to do so. That sounds unpleasantly familiar.

It is all very well to say that conditions have changed, that the safeguards set up to protect freedom are now barriers to progress, and that in these enlightened days they can be dispensed with.

Conditions may have changed, but human nature has remained unchanged.

Men are still ambitious for political power over their

fellow men; and it is a sobering sight to see how, under the domination of ambition and the lust for personal power, ancient tyrannies reappear as soon as the safeguards are swept aside.

The blood purge that took place in Germany some two years ago has its exact counterpart in the Florence of the Medicis. The modern concentration camps are nothing more than the revivals of the Bastille, where men were sent by executive order, and without benefit of trial. The present-day persecution of racial and religious minorities, deprived of the protection of the law, is but a reversion to the practices of the Middle Ages.

If men are to remain free, safeguards are as necessary today as they ever were. If not, then why have the modern dictators found it necessary to destroy every one of them.

Extreme centralization of power in Washington involves another danger.

It makes our governmental system increasingly vulnerable to the pressure of organized minorities whose interests may not be in the best interests of the nation as a whole. There are already extraordinarily strong blocs whose leaders are fully aware of their political power.

In the first instance, the danger is that these blocs, each acting for its own selfish interests, may collectively so load down the economic organism that it can no longer function. When this happens, the government will take over.

Alternatively, one minority group becoming supreme might ruthlessly exploit other minority groups, as well as the unorganized majority. Under such circumstances, control of government would become a matter of economic life or death to whole sections of the country. Elections would degenerate into desperate battles for political power, in which the Union might well perish. Or, by a supreme effort the government might bring the blocs under control and incorporate them into the legal framework of a new order. A Fascist State would be born.

My primary purpose, however, is not to expose the weaknesses and defects of a collectivist system, or even to point out the dangers that threaten our American civilization.

My purpose is to consider objectively whether our traditional system of free government, of free enterprise, and of individual liberty is capable of satisfying the legitimate demands and aspirations of the people.

If it is, no right-thinking American will ever submit to collectivism and its coercion.

CHAPTER III

A FREE SOCIETY

WE NOW turn from the consideration of what we do
not want in government to the more congenial task of
determining what we do want.

Let me begin with the statement of basic principles
and objectives. In doing so, I want to quote from Professor Hoffman's "Will to Freedom": "When we come
to set down a statement of the conditions necessary to
the prospering of human nature, the first condition to
be named is liberty. Yes, liberty, that goddess whose
shrine is so deserted today. If politics ever become
rational again there will once more be a votive offering
in her temple. The first political principle then will be
the philosophic doctrine of the freedom of the human
will, and the state will find its whole raison d'être in
securing to men that freedom which is required for the
exercise of all the faculties of their nature. Because
man is a rational being, the state will secure his intellectual liberty; because he is a moral being, the state
will protect his freedom of conscience; because he is an
economic being, the state will safeguard the ownership
of productive property; because he is a social being,
the state will protect his right of association. * * *
Because private property is a necessary foundation for

37

individual liberty, it will be defended * * *; because the family is a necessary training school of liberty, it will be protected in every possible way; because religion is a necessary discipline for liberty, it will not merely be tolerated but the freedom of all forms of it which actually serve that end will be most scrupulously respected."

Such a government cannot be content with merely negative duties. Whenever the welfare of society demands its intervention it will intervene; or whenever it is necessary to maintain equality of opportunity; or to protect the weak from the strong; or to preserve free competition; or to meet those responsibilities toward the less fortunate which modern society has decided to assume.

Legitimate intervention, far from curtailing freedom, actually enlarges its boundaries. Wise labor legislation, for instance, does not deprive the worker of his liberty, in a true sense. It protects rights and opportunities that might otherwise be denied him.

In asserting the duty of government to intervene whenever the common welfare demands it, I would place three broad restrictions on the scope of its intervention.

Governmental activities should never assume such dimensions as to entail an unbearable burden of taxation. It is quite possible so to load down the productive organism that it can no longer function. It is quite possible, under the guise of taxing income, actually to divert to unproductive use the flow of capital essential to productive purposes. It is quite possible so to curtail reward as to destroy initiative, ambition and enterprise. We are in danger of doing all of these right now.

Secondly, the activities of government must never be such as to destroy the flexibility and adaptiveness of the economic system. This is what the N.R.A. did.

Third, they must never be such as to encourage dependence and to destroy individual self-reliance, responsibility and character. Such a tendency is definitely visible in some of our present-day policies.

No better scheme of government than ours was ever devised to assure to the individual the widest measure of liberty consistent with the rights of others, and at the same time vest government with authority adequate to protect and to promote the common interests.

It was founded for two great purposes: (1) To establish self-government and (2) to perpetuate the blessings of liberty.

Self-government is assured by representative institutions, popular elections and short tenure of office.

The majority rule, but within the self-imposed limitations in a written Constitution—and never in disregard of the rights of minorities.

The division of powers within the governments makes for a government of laws and not of men.

States' rights and the principle of home rule not only give due recognition to diversity of conditions and interests, but to the necessity of intimate popular supervision and control.

Fundamental human rights are guaranteed by a written Constitution and enforced by independent tribunals.

So long as the Constitution stands and the courts are uncorrupted and uncoerced, no American can be deprived of freedom of speech, of press, of assembly, of religion, of education or of contract; his home is secure from unlawful search, his papers from seizure, his property from confiscation.

The charge that such a system is a laissez faire system is sheer hypocrisy. No such policy has existed in this country.

Our Federal and State governments have ever asserted their right to intervene when intervention was necessary. A great body of legislation imposed in factory laws, labor laws, banking laws, pure food and health laws, anti-trust laws, railroad laws, public utility laws; and the existence of such agencies as the Interstate Commerce Commission, the Federal Trade Commission, the Federal Reserve Board, the Federal Securities Commission, labor departments, State and Federal, tenement house and housing commissions and authorities, public service commissions, public health services, and so on *ad infinitum,* all testify to the existence of ample power.

No sensible man denies that semi-natural monopolies such as railroads and public utilities; banking, finance, public market, and trust functions; and, to avoid waste, certain natural resources, must all be regulated. Power to do so exists. Just as the power exists to perform the social duties demanded by the spirit of the times. If there is any question about this, the doubt should be cleared away by some such constitutional amendment as Senator Borah suggests.

It is not lack of power to achieve legitimate ends that bothers some gentlemen. It is the lack of personal and arbitrary power—power which the Constitution in protecting the rights of the citizen wisely denies.

Our government is not perfect. But, being human, neither are we as a people perfect. It is reasonable to say that our governments faithfully reflect the character of the American people. Their strengths and weaknesses are but a reflection of the virtues and failings of those whom they represent.

In the long run, people get just the kind of government their character entitles them to. The American people have ever been an extraordinarily virile, self-reliant, independent and intensely individualistic race. They have developed a form of government suited to —and worthy of—men who insist on freedom as a right, and who demand nothing more of life than opportunity.

Changed conditions and new problems may impose new duties on government and different methods in the performance of old ones. But so long as the character of our people remains unchanged, the essential character of their government must, too, remain unchanged. Let us continue to be ourselves. Let us not become servile imitators of those with whose traditions and outlook we have nothing in common.

The same is true of our economic system. There is no other system consistent with democratic institutions.

Its main characteristics are:

1. A dynamic quality derived from the energies of countless individuals operating in a free field, and actuated by normal aspirations and ambitions.

2. The competitive process which, by exerting unremitting pressure, compels growth, change and progress.

3. The practice of saving, which assures the constant flow of capital into productive enterprise to replenish other capital that is constantly dissipated through the march of progress.

4. The price mechanism, described in our last chapter. It directs labor and capital into the right channels, thus aiding in bringing demand and supply into balance.

These four forces—the creative impulse of the individual, the pressure of competition, the free flow of capital, and the price mechanism—all serve the primary purpose of increasing efficiency in production and distribution. Efficient production means lower costs. Lower costs, under competitive conditions, mean lower prices. Lower prices bring goods within the purchasing range of more and more people. This results in widening markets. When more and more people can buy more and more of what they need and want, their standard of living goes up. As the market becomes broader and broader, abundance makes its appearance. Poverty tends to disappear.

If, as one of the Marxist liberal writers said, the profit-making motive demands lower wages, inferior general conditions in industry, a diminution of the charges imposed upon capital by taxation and a consequent contraction of the social services, I, for one, would reject any such system of capitalism as fatally defective.

Such has not been our experience with our American system.

To see what our economic system is capable of, let

us take the years of 1899 and 1929. Eliminating price changes, the purchasing power of total national income in 1929 was 140 per cent. greater than in 1899. During the same period, population increased 62 per cent. The number of those gainfully employed increased 69 per cent. Thus the rise in income was much more rapid than the increase in the number of consumers. The rise in income was faster than the number of persons normally employed.

At the same time, the proportion of national income going to wage-earners and salaried employees rose from 53 per cent. in 1909 to 65 per cent. in 1929.

According to Professor Wilford I. King, "employees of the United States were able to purchase with their combined wages and salaries nearly twice as many goods in 1927 as they could have bought in 1909."

Or, as the National Industrial Conference Board tells it: "As compared with 1899, the average amount of money received by wage-earners as a whole for one hour of work was 226 per cent. higher. * * * During the same period the retail prices of a representative group of goods and services bought by wage-earners, as measured by the index of the cost of living, increased 122 per cent., indicating an improvement in the purchasing power of an hour's work of 47 per cent. for wage-earners as a whole."

During the same period the average number of hours worked per week in all occupations declined between 10 per cent. and 15 per cent., and in manufacturing from 56 hours to 48 hours per week.

Examples could be multiplied, but we do not need statistics to prove that private enterprise has raised the standard of living of the American working man above that known to any similar group in history.

This does not mean that there are not many million families in the United States whose incomes are far below what they should be. The raising of the standard of living of these families is our supreme problem —but it is a problem that cannot be answered by merely dragging off the top. What we must do is to lift —not lower.

The only way to do that is to increase the national income as a whole.

The only way to increase the national income is to produce more goods and services.

It should be obvious—although it does not seem to be—that the more goods there are to divide, the greater is the general well-being; the fewer the goods to divide, the poorer the people.

That is why such measures as the thirty hour week will injure rather than help. It may come some day. I do not know. But I do know we are not ready for it.

As the Brookings Institution says in its most recent report: "As an outgrowth of the unemployment situation, there has recently been evolved a policy regarded by its exponents as of vital significance to labor. It is enunciated as a definite principle that working hours should be reduced at the present juncture sufficiently to absorb the existing unemployment, and that henceforth they should be systematically reduced in proportion to increases in productive efficiency. What would be the economic results of such a policy upon living standards and what would be its bearing upon recovery?

"If the principle of reducing hours in proportion to increases in productive efficiency had been in operation between 1900 and 1929, it would have meant that all of the gains resulting from the increase in productive efficiency would have had to be realized in the form of greater leisure—none in the form of higher standards of living. If such a plan were to be put into operation now, with a view to absorbing existing unemployment, it would mean that the volume of national production would be frozen at its present low level—concretely, at about $470 per capita. If the principle of reducing working hours in the future in direct proportion to increasing efficiency were adopted and enforced, there could henceforth be no increase in production per worker or in living standards.

"The advocates of this principle are apparently quite unconscious of its implications from the standpoint of production. The confusion of mind arises from concentration of attention upon money income to the exclusion of everything else. What is seen is that if the working week is shortened sufficiently to absorb unemployment, but without any reduction in weekly wages per person, the total volume of money flowing to the laboring population would be increased. What is not seen is that the expenditure of this increased money income in the markets would not bring forth any larger volume of goods and services—since the very process by which the increased volume of money income is made available prevents any increase in production. We would have on the one side an increasing flow of money into trade channels; but on the other side a flow of goods and services of unchanging magnitude. The certain outcome would be rising prices. By the very nature of the plan, real income—in terms of goods and services—would have to remain stationary. Labor would merely obtain increased leisure.

"It is also assumed that this plan assures, in any event, a more 'equitable participation in the output of industry.' Even the most 'equitable' distribution of a fixed and limited national income of 60 billion dollars would not enable labor to obtain any significant increase in real wages. If the profits of 1936 were completely diverted to employees, the increase accruing to each working-class family would be less than $150. It is, moreover, by no means certain that the plan would lead to an increase in wages at the expense of profits. The rise in prices might leave profits much the same as before."

So it is that the hope of the present low-income group lies in abundance.

Abundance comes from new invention and methods, from the ability of individuals to apply their talents and energies, from the capital essential to vitalize old enterprises and to give birth to new ones. Change and growth are inseparable from progress.

Though relevant, the consideration of such questions as technological progress and unemployment, the distribution of wealth and the existence of large fortunes, is not essential to the development of our main theme. I mention them simply to indicate that I am not overlooking them.

So far as technological unemployment is concerned, the introduction of a labor-saving device does, locally and temporarily, result in a shift of labor. But in the sixty years ending in 1930—the period of the greatest technological advance—the percentage of those gainfully employed did not decrease. It increased.

The charge one often hears, that 2 or 5 or 10 per cent. of the people hold 80 per cent. of the wealth, has no statistical evidence to support it. We have no reliable statistics as to wealth distribution. Income distribution presents a very different picture from that of the alleged distribution of property. It is estimated that in 1926, in terms of 1913 dollars, 83.3 per cent. of the national income went to those with incomes of $5,000 or less.

These are probably the facts. There are many millions of our citizens—a higher percentage than in any other country—who have acquired estates in land, savings deposits, in securities and in insurance. There are altogether too many—and this is particularly true after the long depression—who have no property.

This much we know, however, that only a short time ago there were ten and one-half million families living in urban homes, which they owned, valued at thirty-eight billions; three and one-half million farmers, operating their own farms, valued at twenty-one billions; three million retired farmers that leased their farms, valued at another twenty-two billions; some eight million Building & Loan shareholders with eight billions of assets; twenty million owners of automobiles, valued at eight billions; twenty-four million registered security holders, with securities valued at seventy-six billions; forty-four million individual savings banks depositors, with deposits totaling twenty-four billions; and sixty-three million individual life insurance policy holders, with equities aggregating eighteen billions.

Granting that there is a great deal of duplication in these figures, on the face of it some two hundred fifteen billion dollars worth of property were in the hands of some 91 per cent. of the adult population.

What of large fortunes? Since men are not born with equal abilities, in any free society some are bound to be more successful than others. In the United States the rewards of success have been very great. In respect of large fortunes two points should be noted. First, if we except speculative gains and the accumulations resulting from unfair and predatory practices, new fortunes come into being only through the production or creation of new wealth. Second, under modern conditions the owner of the wealth must share its benefits with others, or get no benefits himself. A factory is not worth anything unless it produces what others want. They share the benefits. It cannot be operated without raw materials. The producers of raw material share the benefits. The wage-earners who operate the plant share them.

Thus, most of the money paid by the consumer goes not to the owner of the wealth, but to those who help him produce. Over the eleven year period beginning in 1919, all corporations in the United States paid out as operating expenses 96 cents out of every dollar of gross income received. They retained but 4 per cent.; and a good part of the 4 per cent. had to go back into plant and machinery.

This free society of ours does not look for cohesion

and purpose to the coercive power of government. It exists—and can continue to exist—only by virtue of a common agreement that a certain social pattern is desirable. Its vitality depends upon the existence of indispensable qualities, and upon the willingness of its members to conform to the necessary conditions.

First among the qualities is self-reliance, and ability voluntarily to unite with others in a spirit of mutual helpfulness and of self-help.

America has been created not by its government, but by its people, acting for the most part within the boundaries of their cities, counties and states. This immense country of ours could never have been built and developed on any other basis—that basis being a sense of community responsibility in a voluntary cooperative effort, without any cement of government coercion.

Secondly, I cannot conceive of a free society in which men do not have a profound feeling of responsibility to their neighbors. If every man is actuated solely by personal selfishness—indifferent to the rights of others and uninterested in their fate—it will not be long before the policeman has to be called in in the name of common decency. Once we must be compelled to live up to our obligations, then we do enter the field of coercion and abandon the field of freedom.

I may be wrong, but I do not believe that this sense of responsibility to one's neighbors can ever be strong and enduring if it rests on a purely ethical basis. I am convinced that it must derive its strength and compelling quality from the spiritual force of religious faith. In other words, I do not believe that the America we know would ever have existed if we had not been an essentially religious people.

Any weakening of religious ties must be a matter of serious concern to friends of a free society.

In the third place, we have recognized that there is a natural order in the conduct of human affairs. That natural order demands that nothing should be transferred to the larger unit which can adequately be performed by the smaller. It begins with the family and the responsibility to care for his own placed upon his head. It extends to the village, with its set of duties, the municipality, the county, the state and, last of all, the national government. Being distant, it is not permitted to direct and govern the life of the individual.

This diversity of authority is what we know as the principle of Home Rule. It is based on the knowledge that the closer the government to the people, the better the government, because power divorced from the source of authority soon becomes irresponsible. Home rule is the cornerstone of free institutions, which the founders of this nation well recognized.

Next we come to leadership. Dictatorships look to one man; aristocracies to the few. Each reduces the people to a level of mediocrity. Men of intellect and character, with qualities of leadership, are not wanted. They become inconvenient, and must be suppressed, even at the cost of progress and enlightenment.

In a democracy there is constant need for leaders in all fields of activity. These are drawn from the ranks of the people. They rise through merit, and their ranks are constantly replenished from the same source. They are the men and women to whom we must look for progress in the arts, and sciences, in professions, in industry, in trade, and in the life of the community.

The men who established our government never contemplated a leaderless society. When they turned their backs on kings and the hereditary aristocracy, they looked to the people to develop their own leaders. When they decentralized the power of government, they expected those leaders to be found in the several communities. When they limited the power of government and relied on the self-reliance and cooperative spirit of the citizens, they anticipated that leadership would not be confined to the sphere of politics.

Their expectations have been realized. We have had leadership. In the main, it has been local leadership. During the greater part of our national life, Washington counted but little in the life of the average family. In the day-to-day task of building a nation, local leadership was what counted most. Nor, in the main, has it been political leadership. In an economically-minded nation, energetic and ambitious men have leaned more to business and the professions than to politics. In every community there are to be found these so-called leading citizens. Leading in what sense? In the sense that because of their achievements, their ability, their judgment and, above all, their character, the community turns to them for leadership and direction. And they, in turn, respond in terms of time and service.

They, too, are vital elements in a free society.

Those who would have us mistrust merit, and suspect success, are not the friends of such a society. There is no more deadly foe to human welfare and progress than the cult of mediocrity.

At the same time, those who are successful and who attain wealth and economic power are not free to use them selfishly or unscrupulously, but with an ever-present sense of public responsibility.

Fifth, anti-social acts and unfair practices through which men seek to profit illegitimately at the expense of their fellows must be stamped out, not only by statutory penalties, but by an aroused public conscience. Business men, for instance, must police themselves. Public opinion and social ostracism are powerful weapons to compel decent behavior.

Sixth, a free society should be a proprietary society, in the sense of a wide diffusion of property ownership. A great majority of men and women must have a direct stake in the existing order, and a corresponding interest in its preservation.

I do not mean that we should endeavor to return to the days of handicraft and of the individual artisan, as has been suggested by a number of writers. We cannot afford to sacrifice all of the immense benefits of mass production. But we must do all in our power to encourage home ownership, farm ownership and the growth of small business enterprises.

We must use to the full the weapon of competition to break up large uneconomic units and undue concentration of economic power. Even today, after a period of industrial concentration, according to the Twentieth Century Fund, more than 81 per cent. of our entire economic activity is carried on by partnerships and individuals, and by small and medium-sized corporations.

We must make the main effort, however, through the income side. When men and women have more than enough to provide necessities and the first comforts, they begin to save. They may buy their home, or a farm, or go into business for themselves, or acquire a savings account, or purchase securities or life insurance. They become proprietors.

The problem is so to raise the income of the lower income groups that those who have the desire and will to save may do so.

As already stated, the first essentials are increased production, increased productive efficiency, and the passing on of the benefits in such a way as to raise real wages by lowering prices. There are other influences that can help toward this attainment. Protection against sweat-shops—stabilization of employment—lower taxes, and such relief from the support of dependents as will be afforded by social legislation, will all contribute.

The objective is clear. It will not be attained in a day. Our job is to see that we move steadily toward it.

Finally, the complete integrity of the competitive process is vital. Government must suppress monopoly, combinations in restraint of trade, price fixing, agreements to suppress competition, and all other monopolistic practices.

This is fundamental in our whole philosophy.

1. Because competition and the price mechanism are the life blood of the economic system.

2. To keep open the door of opportunity.

3. To promote the productive efficiency which assures progress.

4. To pass on the benefits of increased efficiency to consumers as the surest approach to the diffusion of prosperity and increased productivity.

5. To prevent unhealthy and uneconomic concentration of wealth and of power.

If in recent years we had kept our grip on these realities, we would not be in the critical position we find ourselves today.

Under such a social organization, to expect the Federal Government to solve the problems of the individual is ridiculous. There can be no responsibility without corresponding authority. To solve the problems of the individual, the central government has to control his actions, thus transforming a free society into a collectivist one.

If we do not go quite so far as direct responsibility for the welfare of the individual, but look for a system of what Colonel Leonard Ayres calls, "managed economics," that is, "one in which the government controls the volumes of output of the principal products, and the conditions of hours and wages of the workers," this likewise calls for revolutionary changes in our institutions, leading at a slower pace to the same inevitable end.

Planning of this character is progressive and tends to include an ever-widening field of activities. The government restricts the planting of cotton; the farmer turns to peanuts. The government restricts peanut growing; the farmer increases his potato crops. Until finally it becomes a crime to grow more potatoes than the government allows. The whole economic organism is so intimately connected that control at one point inevitably entails successive controls at almost all points.

New rigidities appear, the economic system loses its flexibility; the more the government plans, the more impossible it becomes for individuals to calculate the effects of official acts and to make their own plans. Selfishly interested groups use political pressure to achieve their ends regardless of general economic consequences. And the more the economic machine bogs down, the more deeply the government becomes involved. Having undertaken the responsibility for economic conditions and for the solution of economic problems, it cannot let go—even if it were willing to relinquish its new powers, which is unlikely.

This too is the road to collectivism and dictatorship.

I submit that what we want can be attained—and more surely attained without the destruction of fundamental values.

One may well ask, then, what do we want?

1. Peace, for war means destruction and chaos.

2. Opportunity for each, no matter what his condition, to achieve and to progress in accordance with his inclinations and abilities.

3. A standard of living sufficiently high to establish general well-being, with an always widening opportunity for leisure, recreation and spiritual development.

4. Increased security and protection.

5. Adequate care for those unable to provide for themselves.

6. A more stable existence, free alike from the peaks of illusory prosperity and the very real valleys of temporary depression.

I hope in the remaining chapters to show that the attainment of these ideals is entirely consistent with the continued existence of our free society. Having come along the road this far, who is it who says we can go no further?

CHAPTER IV

THE PRECISE FORM OF THE PROBLEM

I NOW want to discuss the precise form the problem assumes in the United States.

Let me repeat that the whole New Deal movement is an effort to transform an individualistic into a collectivistic society.

The essence of the process is the concentration of power and the assumption of arbitrary authority. Both are part of the mechanics of collectivism.

It follows—and I cannot make this too emphatic—that the defense of freedom demands the maintenance, in its full integrity, of our system of checks and balances, and of our Federal form of government. It is the only form of government that, without sacrificing self-government, civil liberty and individual responsibility, can hold together a great population in an immense country.

Speaking at Williamsburg, ten years ago—and long before the present controversy had arisen—on the occasion of the one hundred and fiftieth anniversary of the adoption of the Virginia Resolution of Independence, I said:

As I read our history, the safety and strength of our institutions is due not so much to the powers granted to the

Federal Government as to those reserved to the States, the very principles upon which the Virginia Convention was so insistent, to the jealousy with which the home rule principle was safeguarded, to the regard held by the Founders for the truths that the closer the government is to the people, the better the government, and that the best way to strengthen and foster self-government is to build up self-reliance and independence in the individual citizen by placing on him direct and intimate responsibility. If this were true when there were but thirteen States, when our inhabitants numbered only some three million, when our population was homogeneous and had, generally speaking, an economic solidarity and that common view which can only be found in a population almost wholly addicted to agricultural pursuits, how much more necessary is it today, when our country has expanded to its present colossal proportions, when its population is made up of races drawn from all parts of the world, with totally dissimilar ancestry, tradition and viewpoint, when within our borders may be found every form of economic activity from the simple agricultural community to the largest of commercial and industrial units, and when a variety of climates necessarily produce different habits, customs and modes of living? That a nation so composed and situated can develop a single and ardent national spirit, a common purpose and ideal, and can embody a great national soul and conscience, has been amply demonstrated by our history. But that this nation, with such a tradition as we've noted, with its characteristics of initiative and love of freedom, true not only of the individual citizens, but of our individual communities, can ever be made uniform by law, and governed from a single, distant centre, is something to me inconceivable. And Washington is far off, in spite of railroads, aeroplanes, and long distance telephones—far off in the sense that it is well nigh impossible for the individual to scrutinize and understand from day to day and from month to month the complexities of its already huge government.

The American principles of ordered freedom, individual rights and responsible government are eternally secure in the safe keeping of forty-eight sovereign governments directly responsive to the rule and supervision of their citizens. To entrust them to one central authority is to hazard their very existence, for, deprived of that sense of personal responsibility in the individual from which they draw their strength, and removed from that jealous vigilance which should constantly attend them, they will gradually lose their strength and grow pale, until the shadow, rather than the substance, remaining, they may be blown away by the first tempest.

Everything that has happened since has but served to confirm this opinion. And let there be no doubt as to the violence of the storm.

Two determined groups at present give impetus to the centralization movement: those public officials who believe in the superiority of collectivism over individualism; and those selfish minorities, without the government, that are fully alive to the possibilities of direct pressure applied to a single center of authority.

Both groups advance the argument that, contrary to the conditions prevailing in an earlier age, commerce, industry, agriculture and labor are all national in scope and character, and must, therefore, be subject to national authority.

We are told we must change our institutions to conform to existing realities.

But are they realities? I say they are not. I say this not because the Constitution as interpreted by the Supreme Court says so. I say it because they are not realities in fact.

An individual farm is not a national enterprise; a factory serving local needs is not; department stores are not; if we except chains, retail establishments are not; hotels, apartment houses and office buildings are not; the building trades are not; with the exception of long distance transportation, public utilities are not; for the most part, mining is not; outside of transportation, communications and some amusements, services are not. Certainly the lives of the fifty million people gainfully employed are governed by the conditions prevailing in their immediate neighborhood.

Conditions of life differ in country and city, in village and town, and even in the great cities. Life in San Francisco differs from that in New York, or in Chicago, or in New Orleans. Prices are not uniform, rents are not uniform, nor are costs of living as well as standards and modes of life. All these vary from region to region, from community to community.

There is no single problem of labor, of agriculture, of industry, or of prices. There are countless problems, arising from an infinite variety of conditions on an immense continent inhabited by a singularly independent, original and individualistic population.

No one can deny there is an immense volume of strictly local business; that is, business originating and terminating in comparatively small areas. This is true of practically all services. It is true of factories, businesses and farms serving a strictly local market. For example, I operate a large commercial dairy in San Mateo County, California. All of its problems, whether of labor, feed costs, prices and consumer demand, are dependent on neighborhood conditions. These problems are very different from those that would confront me in conducting a similar enterprise in Dutchess County, New York. California dairymen have their troubles, as do those in New York. But circumstances are too different to permit a common solution.

Under the proposed policies of centralized control, all of this immense volume of wholly local business would be regulated from Washington—the farm, the factory, large and small, the little one-man and the big department store, the hotels, the barbers, the boot-blacks, the tailors and the pants pressers.

To call these enterprises national is ridiculous.

There is also an immense volume of business that flows across state lines. Under our highly integrated economic system, division of labor is carried to a fine point, and the goods produced by one set of producers are directly or indirectly exchanged for the goods of other producers over great distances.

If the machinery of government were needed to furnish the whole complicated mechanism of exchange to this second line of business, then Federal intervention would be necessary. But, as we saw in our second chapter, the market and the price mechanism perform this essential function with greater flexibility and efficiency than can any central organism.

The case for Federal control, then, must be based on one, or all, of the following grounds:

(1) That central control is necessary to keep the production of all kinds of goods in balance. This is the basic conception underlying a planned economy, the practicability of which we disposed of in our second chapter.

(2) Or that the mere fact that goods are sold over State lines calls for Federal protection of producers. In so far as conditions of labor are concerned, the automobile worker in Detroit does not care whether the car he works on is sold around the corner in Detroit, or in New York, or in San Francisco. His conditions of labor are determined by the conditions existing in Detroit. The State of Michigan has or should have—through Constitutional amendment, if necessary—all of the authority essential to safeguard those conditions.

(3) In the interest of uniformity, the government should equalize competitive conditions, somewhat on the theory of a protective tariff based on the differences between costs of production. What virtue is there in uniformity? To achieve uniformity would be to deprive us of the immense benefits of the greatest free trade area in the world. Within this area capital and labor may seek the most favorable productive conditions. Within this area, unhampered by artificial barriers, they are free to give one hundred and twenty-seven million people the benefits of productive efficiency. To deprive us of this advantage would be to destroy the foundation of our prosperity.

(4) Or, finally, it may be urged that there is an element of unfair competition, which the Federal Government alone can deal with.

This last argument deserves careful consideration.

What is meant by unfair competition is that exploited labor in one section of the country can destroy decent standards of labor in other sections. With goods flowing freely across State lines, to be sold competitively, conditions in one locality undoubtedly may affect conditions in other localities.

There is a problem. But to admit its existence, is not to admit the necessity of collectivism as a cure.

In the first place, the consequences of interstate competition are not so serious as is alleged. New York for some years has led the way in the field of social legislation. Yet Mr. John A. Fitch, of the faculty of the New York School of Social Work, in a statement prepared for the New York State Legislature, has pointed out that New York has in no way been adversely affected. I quote the summary of his findings:

(a) New York has steadily maintained its position as leading industrial state during the last decade.

(b) In the period 1919 to 1927, New York industries increased their products in terms of value more than any other state in the immediate competitive area.

(c) For all industries combined, the ratio of wages to value of product in New York has been consistently lower than in any of the competitive states but New Jersey.

(d) Value of product per employee for all industries combined is greater in New York than in any other state in the competitive area.

(e) In 10 major industries the ratio of wages to value of product is lower in New York than in any of the competitive states, and in twelve more the ratio is lower than in a majority of these states.

(f) The ratio of wages to value added by manufacture is lower in New York for all industries combined than in any other state in the competitive area.

(g) In fourteen out of the 33 major industries, New York has a lower ratio of wages to value added by manufacture than has any other state in the competitive area, and altogether in twenty-four of these industries it is in a more favorable position than are a majority of the competitive states.

He continues, "all of this indicates, clearly enough, that New York not only has not suffered from its leadership in social legislation, but has achieved under it a margin of advantage over other states."

In the second place, we have not begun to explore the possibilities of compacts between the States. Certainly these are available to minimize the evils of unhealthy competition over a wide area.

In the third place, as the decision of the Supreme Court in the Convict Goods Case demonstrates, the Federal Government can afford ample protection to a State undertaking to end unjust and unwholesome conditions within its borders.

Finally, attempted uniformity in the field of social legislation gives rise to difficulties of its own.

Consider the case of maximum hour and minimum wage laws necessary to protect certain groups of workers from exploitation by an unscrupulous minority of employers. A minimum wage, which might be adequate in a small town, where living costs are low and opportunities for outside earnings exist, would be totally inadequate in New York City. Conversely, the New York minimum might be altogether too high for a semi-rural community.

The argument of our collectivist friends that all they desire is the authority to deal with problems that, once local, have become national in character, will not stand up under inspection.

And this is equally true of the statement that an inflexible Constitution and a hardening of judicial arteries have barred all attempts to meet changing conditions.

In the early days of the Republic, the Federal Government was satisfied to provide essential services, and to assure a healthy environment for business. In the main, such regulations as were desirable in the public interests were left to the States.

But, as conditions became more complex and State laws less adequate to deal with all of them, the authority of the Federal Government was gradually extended.

Thus, nearly fifty years ago the Interstate Commerce Commission was created, to provide regulation of commerce across the boundaries of individual States, and particularly to regulate transportation by railroads. By slow and progressive steps the authority of this Commission has been extended.

A little later the Sherman Act, outlawing monopolies and agreements in unreasonable restraint of trade, was enacted. Then the Clayton Act was passed and the Federal Trade Commission created.

This legislation took cognizance of the expansion and integration of certain types of industry where conditions clearly required mass production and the integration of various coordinating activities. Size was condemned only where size was deemed against public interests or where it was based on unfair or monopolistic practices. Emphasis was placed upon the protection of the small or medium-sized business against absorption or destruction by large units.

If monopolies threaten our system of free enterprise,

the Federal Government has all of the authority necessary to eliminate them. If our social structure is undermined by financial or industrial oligarchies, there are no Constitutional inhibitions, that I know of, to forbid their suppression.

Today we have, to mention but a few of the new agencies and functions: a Federal Securities Commission to supervise the issuance of securities; a Federal Reserve Board to control the volume of credit, and to direct our banking policies; a Federal Power Commission to regulate the interstate transmission of power; a Public Health Service that, in addition to its normal duties, actively promotes better health standards in states and communities; a Reconstruction Finance Corporation to supply credit pretty generally; a Home Owners' Loan Corporation and a Federal Farm Mortgage Corporation to serve the credit needs of farm and home owners; an established system of financial aid to the states to enable them better to perform certain educational and social services, including old age pensions and unemployment benefits; a great public works, road building and flood control program; assistance to our merchant marine and air transportation services; and a Department of Agriculture and Farm Credit Administration that are prepared to render every conceivable assistance to the farmer, including soil conservation, loans on crops, crop insurance and even direct subsidies—all this in addition to what we used to consider the normal functions of the Federal Government.

Here is a formidable list of activities and duties as compared with those of the horse and buggy days. The

Federal Government has not been bound by a Constitutional strait-jacket, nor has it suffered from an inferiority complex. We have travelled far. And we can travel farther as new needs arise.

There is no lack of power to attain legitimate ends. If there were, is it not strange that not one of thirty-one Presidents, over a period of more than one hundred and forty-five years, complained of his inability to serve the people within the framework of American institutions?

Is it not conceivable that the fault lies not with our institutions? The French, you know, have a saying, that only the bad workman complains of his tools.

Let me repeat, there is no lack of power to attain legitimate ends. When there is, we need never fear to amend the Constitution—providing we are careful to preserve the freedom and rights which it guarantees, and the spirit, purpose and ideals which it embodies.

This is where the shoe pinches.

The Constitution is the charter of government of a free nation. "Every part of it," said Hamilton, "is a Bill of Rights."

It would be an impossible charter for a collectivist society—because it forbids collectivism.

No mere amendment will serve the purpose of the collectivists—and none has been presented. They would remake America to suit themselves. And to remake America the Constitution must not just be amended—but destroyed.

Since the Constitution cannot be destroyed directly, it is to be rewritten by a subservient Congress, supported by a packed and servile Court.

At no stage in the proceedings are the people to have any voice in the matter.

For their own protection the people must not permit the Federal Government to reach down to the individual farm and to control the actions of the individual farmer, or to reach down into the shop, the retail establishment, the service trades, and there control wages, conditions of labor, production and prices.

It must not be permitted to, because such control could not assure prosperity; it would only perpetuate poverty.

It could promise stability and security, only at the expense of progress.

It could safeguard the individual, only at the cost of his freedom.

It could be effective, only through the triumph of tyranny.

And, finally, such control must not be permitted because it is unnecessary.

In Chapter Three I said that what men want is:

Peace, for war means destruction and chaos.

Opportunity for each, no matter what his condition, to achieve and to progress in accordance with his inclinations and abilities.

A standard of living sufficiently high to establish general well-being, with an ever widening opportunity for leisure, recreation and spiritual development.

Increased security, and protection from the vicissitudes of life whether attributable to our own limitations or to outside causes.

Adequate care and protection for those unable to provide for or to protect themselves.

A more stable existence, free alike from the peaks of illusory prosperity and the very real valleys of temporary depression.

Having concluded our very general survey of governmental and economic systems, we are now in a position to consider specifically whether the attainment of these ideals is compatible with the continued existence of a free society.

CHAPTER V

PEACE

To LAY the foundations of peace we must understand the causes of war.

If I may generalize, wars may be said to arise from any one of four major causes: from the clash of conflicting civilizations; deep-seated racial antagonisms; the imperialistic ambitions of autocrats and of nations; or from economic rivalries and pressures.

We are not interested in the first two of these causes. They are unrelated to the subject matter of these lectures. But may I say that the threat of war, even from these causes, is minimized where men are free.

The danger of war originating either in imperialistic ambitions or in economic maladjustments is something we are interested in. For the danger is greatly enhanced by the very nature of autocratic governments and of planned economies. They make war inevitable.

Generally speaking, human society consists of three elements—a world community, some sixty sovereign nations, and the individuals who compose them.

In our quest for peace we must look to one, or all, of these elements. It is pertinent, therefore, to inquire to which of the three we may look most hopefully—the world community, the nation, or the individual.

There is no doubt but that the world community has everything to lose and nothing to gain from war. The World War demonstrated that modern warfare inflicts intolerable hardship, not just on part, but upon all of mankind. Victors, vanquished and neutrals, one and all, were engulfed in the universal disaster. Even when wars are limited in extent, the gains of one nation are offset by the losses of the other, while the rest of the world suffers from the strain and from the disturbance to trade and commerce.

But in its present state of development the world community is not intimately enough organized to assure peace. To say this is not to dismiss the possibility as imaginary. As has been well said: "Our era has made the Earth as small as the France of Napoleon for the commerce of goods, and as small as the Athens of Pericles for the commerce of ideas." It is not visionary, therefore, to hope that in time, given vision and common sense, the nations may become so intimately united by bonds of mutual interest as to make the disruption of world society by war unthinkable.

This ideal is still distant.

While the world community is always the loser, nations have in the past, and may again in the future, benefit from war.

In the first place, the strong can profit at the expense of the weak; and the temptation is ever present in powerful nations so to enrich themselves. The wars waged by Japan and Italy are all too recent examples of such predatory conflicts.

Secondly, nations unjustly treated as the result of former losing conflicts may look upon violence as a justifiable means of redressing their wrongs.

Finally, there is too long a tradition of war as a legitimate weapon. There are too many age-long rivalries, antagonisms and hatreds, to permit us to place too great a reliance on the nation as a champion of peace. And there is too strong a tendency for men acting collectively as a nation—in the name of patriotism —to do what, as individuals, they would condemn.

We turn, finally, to the third element in human society, the individual.

If we except military and political leaders, the individual can gain nothing from war. On the contrary, he has much to lose. Nations make war, but individuals do the fighting. It is they who are killed and maimed and blinded. It is they, as non-combatants, who suffer agonizing anxiety for those they love—and lose. It is they who always pay the bills, and bear the heavy load of reconstruction.

The individual has every reason to loathe and to dread war. Every rational individual does.

This does not mean that he will not fight, voluntarily and valiantly, when his rights are assailed, or his country invaded, or his vital interests threatened. He will even fight from much less worthy motives.

However, when uninfluenced by propaganda or not subject to adverse pressures from the outside, or when his patriotism is not aroused by some particular issue, the individual in one nation has no occasion to hate or mistrust the individual of another nation. For illustration, what individual American hates the individual

Canadian? Were it not for past conflicts, why should the individual German hate or mistrust the individual Frenchman, or the individual Frenchman the Italian, or the individual Italian the Englishman? Many are united by ties of personal friendship, others by business connections. Still others are drawn together by a common interest in the arts, the progress of science and the pursuit of learning. Travel and personal contacts bring about a better understanding.

There is such a thing as the brotherhood of man. When unhampered by governments, the commerce of goods and the commerce of ideas know no boundaries. Left to themselves, men will play, work and study together. They will trade and do business with one another. And the more they do, the harder it becomes to make them kill one another.

Moreover, man is not simply a material creature, subject to material fears, wants and interests. He is a spiritual being. He has a soul and a conscience. The moral aspect of war has on him an influence from which such impersonal elements as the nation, or the world community, are largely, if not entirely, free.

The individual, then, is the one certain element that can be counted on, both from a material and from a moral standpoint, to treat war as a disease that must be destroyed.

But to make his influence supreme, the individual must be free. If his conscience is to be drugged and his judgment to be clouded by propaganda; if a false nationalism and racialism are to stir his spiritual impulses; if he is to have no voice in choosing the path of war or the path of peace; if the mobilization order of an irresponsible dictator can march him to destruction, then he is lost to the cause of peace—and the cause itself is lost.

Where democracy prevails and men control their own destinies, the full weight of the individual's moral and practical aversion to war is thrown on the side of peace. No one suspects the people of the United States, of France and of England of entertaining anything but peaceful aims.

The present armament race, which is heading the world straight for war, originates immediately in the spirit, purpose and policies of autocrats. Having destroyed liberty, they now threaten civilization with destruction.

Admitting that some of these countries have just grievances and that grave economic policies confront them, even so, the very nature of these dictatorships is a threat to peace. Dictators fan the flames of resentment. They preach an intense and narrow spirit of racialism and nationalism. They glorify war and the military psychology. Their economic policies are those of a General Staff. Their ideal and aim is the nation in arms; and they stimulate their victims with the hope that hardships at home will be rewarded by triumphs abroad. As Napoleon said to his lean and hungry legions, "Over the Alps lie the fertile plains of Italy."

All of these are their stock in trade, the very basis of their existence.

There they stand, matches in hand, before the powder magazines of their own creation, threatening to touch them off should the world deny their demands.

It is a threat that is all the more ominous since self-preservation at home might demand desperate adventures abroad.

Thus it is that a free society under democratic institutions makes for peace * * * and a collectivist society under autocratic leadership makes for war.

This conclusion is reenforced when we examine the respective economic policies of the two systems.

As I said in the first chapter, the century, which witnessed the spread of democratic ideals and the development of free enterprise, likewise saw an immense expansion of international trade and of intercourse between nations. World trade tended to double every thirty years.

I do not mean to suggest that free trade prevailed throughout the world. It did not. While England, one great democracy, followed such a policy, another great democracy, our own, in the main believed in protection.

But the close control of commerce by government, which had characterized previous periods, and all of the arbitrary regulations that went with it, had been abandoned. What was known as mercantilism had disappeared. Tariffs existed. But international trade can and does adjust itself to tariffs. It cannot, and does not, adjust itself to quotas, embargoes, exchange restrictions, currency depreciation, and the whole present-day mechanism of control.

Granted that conditions were propitious, the simultaneous growth of democracy, free enterprise and international trade was no coincidence. Rather was it a characteristic of a society growing increasingly free.

Where men are free to do what they want, go where they want and invest where they want, their economic activities are not confined to one country.

No country produces all that it needs. The mere satisfaction of their countries' wants will lead them abroad. Enterprise, ambition and the hope of reward will carry them to the far corners of the earth.

As countries in the satisfaction of mutual needs trade with each other, as goods, capital and enterprising men move freely across national boundaries, the mechanism of the market-place becomes world-wide, with world business transacted with the speed and facility of domestic business.

International trade, growing for the benefit of all, is what makes for peace.

First. It builds up a mutuality of interest among the nations, No one wants to destroy a customer.

Second. It promotes general prosperity, and prosperity is the enemy of war.

Third. And this is most important. It enables the nations less blessed with natural resources to sell what they have to secure what they need.

The doctrines of self-sufficiency and of completely controlled national economies present a radically different picture.

Both are characteristic of present-day collectivism.

The desire for self-sufficiency in many cases arises from the fear of war and the consequent cutting off of essential supplies. In turn, the development of self-sufficiency calls for national economic planning and control.

On the other hand, a planned economy, in the sense

of government control of production, is one of the cardinal principles of the collectivist faith. It is evident that effective control of production at home calls for a like control of imports and exports. Moreover, the insulation of the domestic economy from foreign contacts and influence greatly facilitates the carrying out of a planned program. A prime essential in the development of economic planning by government is the isolated State.

As a consequence, the doctrine of self-containment and self-sufficiency quite naturally emerges as a corollary to the conception of a planned economy.

Though they may try to, all nations cannot become self-sufficient. In fact, very few can. This is true because raw materials were distributed by nature without regard to the political frontiers created by man. Even we, richly endowed as we are, must import our tea from the Orient, our coffee from Brazil, and most of our sugar from Cuba. We must import our rubber and tin. And, in spite of our great coal and iron deposits, we must buy ore from Sweden to make tool steel for our industries.

Other countries are far more dependent than we upon production outside of their own borders. Many of them must import oil, coal, metals, cotton and even food stuffs. To pay for these they must be able to sell to other countries the raw materials they produce at home or else the articles they manufacture.

Self-sufficiency means the elimination of imports on the part of the self-sufficient country. Remember that one nation's imports are the exports of other nations, and that curtailment of a nation's exports may well deprive it of the means of acquiring the materials and goods it needs from the outside world. And when in turn it curtails its imports, it likewise inflicts the same predicament on other nations.

Viewed this way, self-sufficiency is an act of economic warfare, which, because of its nature, tends to become more and more general. Finding it increasingly hard to sell what it must to buy what it needs, nation after nation, in the name of self-preservation, is driven to adopt many substitutes and expedients. To some nations shy of natural resources this brings hardship, discontent and bitter resentment that find expression in war.

It is held in many quarters that international trade fosters war; that nations fight to capture new markets or to retain old ones. Opposed to this contention is the argument that the monopolization of the supply of raw materials by one or a few nations is far more likely to give rise to armed conflict than does international trade in these same materials. One of the first activities inaugurated by the League of Nations after its founding was a world survey of raw material supplies. The League held that access to and a reasonable distribution of these materials among nations are essential to the maintenance of world peace. I accept this view.

If all governments are to plan and control—if, to facilitate planning, they are to seek self-sufficiency— if international trade is to stagnate—if mutual interests are to disappear—and if the nations are to snarl at each other in envy and hatred from within their self-contained citadels, where else can it all lead but to universal disaster?

The road to peace lies in the opposite direction.

It is the road of individual freedom, of democracy and of mutual intercourse and helpfulness among the nations.

As individuals we can—and we must—uncompromisingly resist every encroachment upon free institutions. If we permit democracy to be betrayed here in the land of its birth, it can easily be that freedom will be doomed everywhere.

As a nation we can cooperate with other nations in relieving the political tension by relieving the economic tension. The arbitrary barriers that impede international trade should one by one be resolutely attacked. But no nation alone can resist prevailing tendencies. Concerted action is urgently needed. It could still be done were there the will to do it. It might call for apparent sacrifice, but this would be a small price to pay in preventing world disaster.

As was recently pointed out in "The Economist":

For seven years the principal countries of the world have been fighting universal economic depression. Their weapons have been forged at home. Home markets in every trading country have been turned by State action during the depression into closed preserves for home producers, both industrial and agricultural. The apparatus which brought about the change has been fastened upon the economic life of every country—crisis tariffs, import quotas, restriction and marketing schemes, subsidies, and State-sponsored monopolies for large vested interests.

The result, after seven years, is that whereas the world's

industrial activity is back at its 1929 level (it should normally have shown a very considerable growth in these past seven years), the volume of world commerce in 1936 was still only a little over four-fifths of its pre-depression magnitude. Today, when unproductive State expenditure on armaments contributes an ever-growing stimulus, every country discovers a certain unbalance in its national economy. In highly protected home markets, for example, people begin to talk of boom conditions. On the other hand, in the sphere that is still conditioned by world economic influences, there are so-called distressed areas, languishing export trades, and redundant industrial or agricultural capacity.

Where has this left the cause of peace?

Some nations seem to have achieved temporary prosperity by such measures as they have adopted; other nations have kept going through the liberal use of government credit. But there are other nations that are engaged in the depressing process of tightening their belts and sharpening their swords. No one knows to what extent such economic activity as exists in these countries is due to government expenditures on armaments.

But this much we do know:

All over the world political despots are inflicting a frightful burden of debt, and of taxation, on their people in preparing for war. Every great nation is feverishly arming—and in not one of them will this year's budget be balanced. How long can such madness continue without an explosion?

Are leadership, statesmanship and reason so bankrupt that the peoples of the world must helplessly await this universal disaster?

Has not the world learned that individual liberty, democratic institutions, free enterprise and commerce among the nations are the only foundations upon which it can build?

It should not be too much to expect that there is someone of power and authority who has the vision and the courage to proclaim and battle for the truth before it is too late.

Would that our country might take the lead—for, surely, these vast sums being spent for destruction could be better spent in mutual helpfulness in the cause of peace.

CHAPTER VI

SECURITY

FUNDAMENTALLY, the problem of economic security is this: How to organize and increase production so that the masses of the people will enjoy regular work and a rising standard of living.

Hand in hand with this part of the problem is the phase of dependency—that is, providing for those who are unable to provide for themselves.

The two problems are closely related. Though dependency also arises from other than economic causes, it is conditioned to a great extent by the adequacy and regularity of wage income. At the same time, since the cost of social insurance must come out of national income, it inevitably lowers the standard of living of those productively engaged.

Although they are closely related, it makes for more convenient treatment if I divide the discussion into two parts: (1) The economic security of those productively engaged; (2) The economic security of those who are dependent.

In considering the relationship of government to those economically active, we may lay down this general principle:

Under modern complex conditions, government must intervene on a broad front for the protection of the individual. But it must not push intervention to the point where it deprives the individual of the essentials of his freedom, breaks down the motivating impulses of a free economy or impairs its mechanism.

Not to exhaust the list of Federal functions and duties, but by way of illustration, I would hold the Federal Government responsible:

For a general environment favorable to economic progress, without weighting the scale in favor of any group, whether agricultural or industrial.

For a sound fiscal policy.

For the encouragement of international trade.

For assuring equality of opportunity by suppressing monopolies, monopolistic devices, unfair and predatory practices, and undue concentration of wealth and of economic power.

For control of interstate commerce; and for the regulation of all public utilities doing an interstate business.

For the supervision of security issues.

For a sound currency and a sound banking system.

For the preservation of natural resources.

For assuring adequate credit facilities to home and farm owners.

For our well-established system of State aid.

For assistance to agriculture along lines within the Federal jurisdiction, which I shall later outline.

To the States I would assign the responsibility for the conditions under which men and women live and labor. Again, by way of illustration:

This means housing laws to ensure minimum standards of safety and of comfort in existing dwellings.

It means higher standards in newly constructed dwellings.

It means state and municipal assistance in slum clearance.

It means factory laws to protect the health, safety and welfare of workers.

It means compensation laws for those who are injured.

It means child labor laws for the safeguarding of youth.

It means maximum hour and minimum wage laws for those unable effectively to protect themselves.

It means protecting the right of association.

It means the suppression of monopoly, of fraud, of predatory practices, of racketeering, and of the stacking of the cards against any individual or group.

Once governments, Federal and State, have done all in their power to provide a healthy environment; to assure decent living and working conditions; to protect the citizen from exploitation; and to guarantee equality of opportunity—then maximum economic freedom will bring maximum economic benefits—not only to exceptional men and women, but to all.

The economic security of those economically active means: (1) Steady employment; (2) A rising standard of living that brings greater comfort today, and more adequate provision for tomorrow.

The most characteristic product of our American system has been a constantly advancing standard of living.

The secret of our success has been that production has regularly increased a little faster than population.

Production means purchasing power, and when purchasing power increases faster than population increases, the standard of living rises.

Increased production was accompanied by increased efficiency in production. That means lower costs of manufacture. Lower costs mean lower prices. Lower prices mean higher real wages, because the same number of dollars in Saturday's pay envelope will purchase more goods. That too means a rising standard of living.

Lower prices also mean that more people can buy. More customers mean more goods produced. More goods produced mean more employment. More production and more employment mean more purchasing power.

The whole process of steady employment and a rising standard of living can be expressed in terms of three inseparable factors: increased efficiency, increased production, and increased employment.

Our free economic system has met these tests, as no other system ever has.

Turning, now, to the second main phase of the problem—that of steady employment—it is alleged:

1. That, whatever may have been true in the past, the present economic machine is incapable of furnishing full employment.

2. That, unless the government intervenes, periodic depressions will deprive millions of work.

As to the first argument, Secretary Wallace said on February third:

We are now close to our 1929 volume of industrial activity, but 8 to 9 million people are still unemployed compared with about 2 million in 1929. We can probably exceed the 1929 level of activity, reach a new level of maximum utilization of capacity and find ourselves with 4 million people still unemployed on the eve of the next business collapse, unless we make sure of balanced progress from now on.

Mr. Wallace was mistaken. The fact is, we were not close to our 1929 volume of industrial activity. The average monthly physical volume of total production and trade in 1936 was about 17 per cent under the average monthly level of 1929. Aggregate employment was approximately 9 per cent under the 1929 average.

In other words, employment has more than kept pace with increased business activity.

Where Secretary Wallace and others err is that they center attention on the number of unemployed, which include, not only the decrease since 1929 in the number of employed, but also the number of new workers who have been added through increase in population.

Since the total number of unemployed—the new workers included—has not been reduced as rapidly as business activity has approached 1929 levels, the inference is drawn that employment has not increased as rapidly as business activity.

From this false premise the further conclusion is drawn that continued recovery cannot absorb the great body of the unemployed; and that they constitute a permanent problem.

There is another side to this story.

The National Industrial Conference Board estimates that, assuming during the next four years the 1933 to 1936 rate of increase in activity and of output per man hour, with the same weekly working hours, there will be an actual shortage of 1,600,000 gainful workers in 1940, after allowing for temporary unemployment due to seasonal operations, sickness, etc.

This appears to be a reasonable estimate. For seven years we have added little to our capital equipment or to our supply of housing. Taking into consideration the need to catch up with normal growth and with the increase in population, there are enormous deficiencies in these two items alone. Once well started, these two could easily absorb the existing labor surplus.

What we face is a probable labor shortage, not permanent unemployment.

So much for the present-day problem of steady employment.

Loss of employment because of periodic depressions demands serious consideration. Economic security is directly related to economic stability. But to recognize this obvious fact is not to admit we need government control to keep the national economy in balance.

Government cannot guarantee balance:

(1)—Because no man, or any group of men, can visualize our manifold economic activities as a whole with sufficient clearness to exercise effective control over them.

(2)—Because government control means political control. And political control means that, at one time or another, some group will exercise an influence sufficiently great to upset the balance.

(3)—Because four years of managed economies have brought us face to face with the dangers of an inflationary boom, to be followed by the inevitable collapse—which, this time, will include the credit of the Government itself.

Let us examine this problem of economic stability.

One all-important fact must immediately be noted. Wars are fatal to stability.

All great wars are followed by major economic depressions. This was true of our Revolutionary War, the Napoleonic Wars, the War of 1812, our Civil War; and now the World War, fought on an unparalleled scale, has been followed by a depression of intolerable scope and intensity.

If there had been no World War, there would have been no world depression.

History from 1873 to 1914, despite immense growth and technological change, gave strong hope that the violence of the swings in the business cycle was being moderated, and that it was possible to prolong the periods of good times and to soften and shorten the periods of reaction.

When the economic system is in balance, there is no evidence of any problem. There is an active demand for capital and labor. Goods clear the markets of one another. Production gives rise to the income which supports consumption. Production and consumption expand together.

If it were not for the changes that occur in a dynamic society, in a free economy the mechanism of price and of the market place would preserve equilibrium, and restore balance when, for one reason or another, it was disturbed. If prices and interests rates correctly reflect underlying conditions of supply and demand in their respective fields, and they move promptly and adequately, even moderate changes will correct maladjustments before they have gone too far.

However, we do live in a society of extraordinarily dynamic character; and our problem is conditioned by this fact.

Innovations and inventions follow one another in rapid succession. New industries and processes arise overnight, only to be succeeded by still newer ones. Tastes, fashions and modes of life change from year to year. Population growth and migration alter trade relationships and develop new markets as human centers of gravity are shifted.

These changes often give rise to psychological waves of optimism and pessimism which express themselves in cyclical fluctuations, frequently aggravated and exaggerated by credit expansions and contractions.

One phase of the cycle develops into another. The impact of initial forces is disseminated throughout the entire economic system. On the upper sweep of the cycle initial increases in prices and profits stimulate further excesses.

All industries, however, do not share alike in the revival. Various strains develop. Interest rates rise. The debt burden increases. Bank credit is substituted for savings and consumers' income. Bank portfolios become clogged with long-term assets. The income of various groups begins to lag. Maladjustments of price and production between various industries appear.

Eventually all these situations become so acute as to call for readjustment. Prosperity passes into crisis and depression.

One thing is certain. There is no single cause of the business cycle. And there is no single cure.

In fact, it is highly doubtful whether the business cycle can be entirely eliminated.

A dynamic society advances by spurts. The railroad building era is followed by the development of the electrical, the automobile and the oil industries. Capital equipment must be provided in advance of actual needs. Capital development involves a rapid increase at one time, to be followed later by a lull.

These spurts generate cyclical fluctuations. They are the growing-pains of a changing economy.

This is true not only of capitalistic, but of socialistic and communistic societies. Russia prides herself on having no unemployment. She is in the development stage of her economic growth. Once the desired capital equipment is provided, she too, if she means to progress, will experience the rhythms of economic life.

It must further be borne in mind that where a whole country constitutes one financial unit, so that losses in one place are covered by profits in another, the relatively minor reactions of a free economy may be eliminated only to pave the way for fewer but far more drastic reactions. Mistaken policies on the part of individual enterprisers are quickly revealed by the balance sheet. Mistaken policies on the part of the whole economy may be hidden and covered over until an appalling deterioration has taken place. Governments can conceal losses and can carry through mistaken policies far longer than a free economy can. Russia has had such episodes. The "New Economic Policy," adopted in 1921, was a reaction from what was virtually a complete collapse in the first policy of the Soviet Government. The "Five-Year-Plan" of 1928, also, was a violent reaction from the preceding policy, which had been using up the accumulated physical capital of the country very rapidly.

Though the cycle cannot be eliminated, much can be done to temper the swing of its fluctuations. The establishment of free competitive markets, refraining from price controls, the elimination of cartels, trusts and combines, the encouragement of international trade, the adoption of sound financial policies will prevent errors from becoming cumulative, and tend to hold cyclical fluctuations within a narrow range.

Money and credit play an activating and aggravating role. The elimination of disturbances from the side of currency and banking would certainly help.

The application of sound financial policies must be made during recovery. The truth in the old statement has often been demonstrated. The only way to mitigate the severity of the depression is "to sit on the boom."

In an able and penetrating article published in the April number of the magazine, "Fortune," Mr. Eccles, Chairman of the Federal Reserve Board of Governors, has outlined measures that can be taken to mitigate the severity of the business cycle.

I am so completely in accord with nearly all of his suggestions, and they are so consistent with the principles that govern a free economy, that I cannot do better than to recite them:

(1) Monetary control through the powers vested in the Federal Reserve authorities, with the cooperation of the Treasury, to control and limit the expansion of reserves, bank loans and investments, and deposit currency, together

with the right given the Federal Reserve System to pre-
scribe margin requirements.

Says Mr. Eccles, "There has never been a prolonged
inflationary period that has not been accompanied and
fed by an expansion of the means of payment."

I agree. I agree too, when he says:

(2) A fiscal policy under which government debt is retired during periods of prosperity, even at the cost of increased taxation.

Though what the present situation calls for is a decrease in cost rather than an increase in taxes.

(3) The development of a flexible public works program,
that can be suspended when the swing is upward, and be
put into effect when the tide turns.

(4) The control of foreign funds that at times flood our
markets; and may be suddenly withdrawn.

While I do not agree with the suggested remedy—
"affecting the value of the dollar relative to other currencies"—, I believe that means must be evolved
through which Central Banks may control the movement of international funds in and out of the domestic
market.

There has been altogether too much loose money
rattling around the world.

I also agree when he says:

(5) The discouragement of labor policies that might result in increased prices and speculative buying; in increased
shortages in individual lines; in losses of total output; and
in reduction of national income.

(6) The reform of our banking system, which repeatedly in the past has proved to be the weak spot in our economic structure.

Says Mr. Eccles, "A major task of banking reform still remains to be done."

(7) Control of security speculation.

This is another dangerous threat to stability. But "the legislation of recent years should do much to correct past abuses, make for a more orderly market, and lessen greatly the danger of wide-spread forced liquidation in the future."

(8) In the case of excessive price rises on particular products in important fields, something of a direct nature might be done by effective anti-trust legislation and by reducing tariffs under the flexible tariff powers.

I part company with Mr. Eccles when he suggests (1) that government through the taxing power can and should apportion the amount of current income to be devoted to saving, and the amount to go into consumption; and (2) that in the face of an inflationary boom interest rates should be kept at an artificially low rate.

As to the first, I do not believe that any government has the wisdom, the knowledge or the experience to make such a decision. This is managed economics all over again.

As to artificially low interest rates, it means the suspension of the regulatory function of interest. It destroys one of the danger signals. It masks the lack of capital and brings about the substitution of bank credit for saving. Thrift is discouraged, speculation encouraged.

Price controls are always dangerous. But never so dangerous as in the case of the rate of interest where the effects permeate the entire economic system.

Throughout this book I have earnestly sought to exclude criticism that might appear to be partisan. But the picture would not be complete if I did not mention the situation that confronts us.

We are faced with an inflationary boom as to the seriousness of which Mr. Eccles at least has no doubts. It could be arrested were there the will to do so. But the will seems to be clearly lacking. Were it not, the first step, balancing the Federal budget, would be taken.

When trouble comes, as it will, where does the blame lie? This time there can be no doubt. The responsibility lies with an Administration that for four years this July sought the easy way of expediency out of every difficulty.

In the reflation of the price level and in the stimulation of business, governmental deficits were to be the activating force. As business increased, these were to taper off. Such was the cyclical theory of public finance. Deficits in depression were to be matched by surpluses in good times.

Well, the good times are here. And the deficit is still about as large as at the bottom of the depression. In the meanwhile, through the medium of bank financing of deficits, there has been injected into the current of our economic life an enormous volume of artificial credit.

Since the middle of 1933 bank deposits have increased by $14,000,000,000, and loans and investments by $11,000,000,000.

This is the most rapid increase in bank credit ever experienced by this country in a comparable period of time. It is a major inflationary factor.

Our dollar was depreciated to the point where it was undervalued in terms of world currencies. As a result, gold has poured in. Member bank reserve balances were increased by $4,000,000,000. Twice member bank reserve requirements have had to be increased. But even so, there were $890,000,000 of excess reserves early in May. They will provide the basis for an additional expansion of credit totaling at least four billion dollars.

Thus, the Administration itself has laid the foundation of the crisis of which it now solemnly warns us to beware.

It is no answer to say that the program seems to have been successful since recovery is here. It must not be forgotten that when this Administration took office, the downswing of a very severe depression had ended. We had suffered, but we had come through with our governmental system intact; our economic organism weakened but unimpaired; and the credit of the government still supreme. There was a firm foundation on which to build and history when written will so record.

Had the Administration followed the orthodox fiscal policies which it first adopted, recovery would have come more quickly, more surely, and more safely.

The example of England confirms this opinion.

We followed instead what appeared to be the painless way. There is a price to be paid, however. We may not think so, but we are going to pay it—pay it in terms of the loss of, what has been most emphasized, —security.

Let me summarize my conclusions:

1. A continuation of our American system of free enterprise holds every prospect of a rising standard of living.

2. There is good reason to believe that steady employment can be expected for the next few years.

3. While cyclical business movements cannot be eliminated in a dynamic society, we possess the technique to mitigate their swings.

4. This favorable picture is marred by the threat of an inflationary boom, resulting from the opportunistic fiscal and monetary policies of the government.

PART II

We turn now to the problem of the security of those who, temporarily or permanently, are unable to provide for themselves.

The community has always taken care of dependents through mutual aid and neighborly assistance, poor laws and private charities.

We have now decided—and I know of no disagreement as to purpose—to perform this duty in a more orderly, dignified and comprehensive way.

And may I say there is no reason why a free society, because of its higher productivity, should not be able to contribute on a more generous basis than a collectivist society.

Dependents must be supported out of what those productively employed produce. There is no other source of supply. Government may give them pieces of paper called money. However, they cannot eat money, clothes themselves with money, or house themselves with it. Money merely gives them a call on all these things. But someone has to produce the food, make the clothes and build the houses. And those who produce these essential goods must produce them in sufficient quantities not only to provide for their own needs, but if dependents are to be cared for, they must produce, also, a surplus adequate to supply the dependents. From which it follows that:

(1) Just as a rising standard of living for the worker depends on increased productivity, so likewise does the welfare of the dependent. We must not, therefore, overburden the productive mechanism or discourage the incentive to produce.

(2) Since they both come out of a common pot—the national income—the more the share of dependents is increased, the smaller the share of the producer, and the greater drag on his standard of living. It is important that he understand this, and that for his protection he may be so taxed as to know the cost. For it is inevitable—and this is one of the penalties of a free society—that the dependent group will endeavor to use their votes constantly to increase their share.

And the demagogues will encourage them.

Other than those long since established, the four accepted methods of providing for dependents are: unemployment insurance; unemployment assistance either through home or work relief; old age pensions;

and Federal aid to the States for the better care of children, the blind, the physically handicapped, and for improved public health.

The last is merely an extension of an established system, and calls for no comment.

As to the other three, we cannot concern ourselves with the details of particular measures. We must confine ourselves to essential principles.

The main question of principle is whether these duties are to be undertaken by the Federal Government or by the States, either on their own or with Federal assistance.

Insofar as old age pensions are concerned, there is the further question as to whether they should be based in part on the insurance principle with the creation of a large reserve, or established on a pay-as-you-go basis supported by a widespread system of direct taxation.

I believe in the establishment of unemployment reserve funds. They furnish a first line of defense to the unemployed worker. They make provision for casual and intermittent unemployment; and, while not supplying absolute security, within limits they do afford greater security than the worker would otherwise enjoy.

I also believe that unemployment reserve systems fall within the jurisdiction of the States rather than that of the Federal Government.

Conditions of employment, wages, standards and modes of life differ widely in different sections of the United States. There is also almost as wide a divergence in the character of the problems of the many diversified local industries. Success is much more likely to be achieved by recognizing these conditions, and permitting the States to solve the problem in accordance with the needs and wishes of their own people, rather than to attempt the application of a single rigid and unified system. To do the latter would be to lose the benefit of experimentation in forty-eight separate laboratories in what, in this country at least, is a new field.

For instance, the report made by the Connecticut Unemployment Commission has not received the attention it deserves. The Commission suggests a dismissal wage as a substitute for the various plans, based on the insurance principle. Its simplicity carries a great appeal. It does away with the whole complicated machinery that has to be set up to check the ability of the unemployed worker to find other work, to determine whether the work is suitable, and to solve other similar problems arising in connection with the termination of benefits.

It is important to realize that the problem of dependency arising out of unemployment is met only in part by any system of insurance. The experience of Great Britain is conclusive on this point.

In other words, side by side with the limited insurance benefits that are paid as a right, there must exist a second line of unemployment assistance, based upon need.

Both from the standpoint of tradition and sound administration, this is a duty of the communities and the States. In normal times the burden will be insignificant. In periods of protracted unemployment the Federal Government should give financial assistance where assistance is needed.

But the present system of Federal administered unemployment relief should be terminated. It should be terminated in the interest of the men and women on relief. They are in danger of becoming isolated from the main stream of our economic life, of living in a little world of their own,—and of being dependent upon a distant government for their daily bread and upon a vast bureaucracy for the direction of their lives.

Unless we are careful, irrespective of opportunities for employment, they may become a permanently isolated group—a group that will become increasingly politically minded and more and more inclined to exert political pressure.

Cared for by the community, or working for the community at tasks approved of by their neighbors, even though temporarily outside the normal economic stream, they will not think of themselves, or be in fact, a class apart.

Moreover, local authorities familiar with local conditions are in a much better position to determine just what form the relief should take. There are always bridges to be built, roads to be repaired, parks to be planted, improved and kept in order. This work has always been a function of the local communities.

Non-political local agencies will administer the taxpayers' money with greater frugality than a Federal bureaucracy; and the taxpayer is in a better position to exercise supervision.

If State legislatures and municipal authorities would create relief funds to be replenished through continuing appropriations in periods of prosperity, and invested in their own securities, it would be a real step forward. The public debt would be reduced in periods of plenty, the governments placed in possession of additional borrowing power for relief purposes in periods of depression, and the necessity of imposing new taxes, when they are least bearable, avoided.

Our present old age pension system provides for two forms of assistance:

1. Aid granted under defined standards of need to any aged citizen, under State administration, with the Federal Government contributing one-half of whatever monthly allowance may be granted up to a maximum of $30.

2. A national system of old age annuities, intended to be completely self-supporting, on an actuarial reserve basis. It contemplates the creation, through contributions from workers and their employers, of an immense reserve fund. It excludes, however, almost half of those gainfully employed, whose occupations are not covered.

The wisdom of setting up side by side two such dissimilar plans is open to serious question.

There is a very strong case for abandoning the system of insurance annuities entirely; and of confining ourselves to grants in aid to the States for assistance to the aged needy, supported by a direct and widely distributed tax on all classes of the population.

This would do away with a so-called reserve fund which is a temptation to extravagance, and adds nothing to security.

The funds collected in the form of payroll taxes must be invested in government bonds. During periods of deficits the Treasury sells its obligations to the Insurance Fund and converts the payroll taxes into the general fund. They then become available for current expenditure of any kind.

Moreover, since the interest on these bonds held in the Insurance Reserve Fund, and their ultimate redemption, depend upon the taxing power of the government, it must be clear that the fund gives no greater security than would the use of the taxing power in the first instance on a pay-as-you-go basis.

The abandonment of the insurance plan would do away with need of keeping enormously costly and elaborate records, along with an enormous and costly bureaucracy.

It would result in greater equity as between recipients of benefits, not only as between the members of the two major groups, but as between annuity payers.

It would make the people as a whole more conscious of the cost.

On the other hand, the European trend seems to be along the lines of developing the insurance program—without the reserve, however—and to utilize the non-contributory system chiefly for transitional and supplementary purposes.

I am not enough of an expert to express an opinion as to which is the best course to pursue.

Let me conclude with a word of caution. We are agreed that society is to increase the economic security of the individual. There is no doubt as to our desire and ability to do so. But it involves two dangers against which we must guard.

We cannot afford to blunt the incentive of the individual to provide for himself, or to weaken the ties of responsibility that bind together the family.

In our search for individual security we must not impair collective security by placing upon our economic organism a burden so heavy as to forbid expansion and progress.

CHAPTER VII

AGRICULTURE

WE HEAR the agricultural problem currently discussed as if it constituted a single problem. There is no single agricultural problem. There are as many agricultural problems as there are agricultural products; as many as there are areas in which they are produced; almost as many as there are farmers. To illustrate:

The cotton farmer is on an export basis. His price is closely tied to the world market. The milk producer is on a domestic basis. His prices react to supply and demand forces operating within our own borders—frequently to purely local conditions. The prices of certain staples, with a relatively constant demand, such as wheat, are determined largely by the supply. The prices of semi-luxuries, such as milk and poultry products, are dependent largely upon demand. They follow closely the volume of factory payrolls.

This is not to say that many of these individual agricultural problems are not closely inter-related, or that conditions and policies affecting one set of producers may not have a direct effect on other sets of producers.

It must be remembered that the farmer is a buyer as well as a seller of agricultural products. High prices favor some and injure others. The grain grower may flourish on high grain prices. The cattle feeder and the dairyman may suffer economic loss because of those same high prices. A prohibitive tax is imposed on the sale of oleomargarine in some states as a protection to the dairyman. This same tax works injury to domestic producers of those fats and oils which go into the manufacture of the taxed product. When the government pays farmers to quit growing certain crops, in reality it pays them to grow other crops, with the result that such action may result in shifting the burden of the depression from one group of growers to another group.

It is clear that agriculture is not a single industry. It is a family of industries. Each member of that family has its own peculiar set of problems. The interests of some members are often in conflict with the interests of other members.

I do not mean to imply that there are no national aspects to farming, or that the Federal Government does not have a direct interest in, and obligations to, agriculture. Quite the contrary, as we shall later see.

What I want to do at the outset is:

First, to direct attention to the impossibility of doing justice to the subject in a single chapter.

Second, to emphasize that here is an industry quite unsuited to control from a single center.

Said Jefferson: "Were we directed from Washington when to sow and when to reap, we should soon want bread."

Third, to point out that there is no occupation to which the doctrine of individualism applies with greater force. By its very nature, agriculture is individualistic.

Here we have no intricate corporate structures; no great aggregations of capital; no mass production.

Though under the gentle rain of cheques he may be temporarily blind to the efforts to collectivize him, the farmer is the supreme individualist. He will be the last among us knowingly to surrender his liberty.

But if he is to preserve his individuality and liberty; if he is not to become a ward of the government; if he is to continue lord of his own farm; he too must accept the mainspring of free enterprise, the competitive principle.

Once comparable efforts are rewarded in agriculture to the same extent as in other industries, the farmer must go ahead under his own power—sink or swim.

For an industry that admits of no sinking is likely to become a dumping ground of cast-offs from other industries, and to lose its vital energy.

Since the founding of this nation, agriculture has contributed generously in man power to industry and to commerce. At the same time, it retained its full share of efficient workers, as attested by the fact that the increased per capita production on the farm has equalled that of the factory. Of recent years the situation has changed. The opportunities in agriculture have not kept pace with those in manufacturing and commerce. It is in the public interest that opportunities on the land again equal those in the city. We want our farms to be peopled with the efficient and alert, and agricultural progress to keep pace with progress in other industries.

I have had some practical experience in farming— that is, in three classes of farming. I know something about apple growing. I know something about the cattle business. I know a great deal more about dairying.

I've learned one lesson in all three branches.

When I have a good apple crop in Dutchess County, so does everyone else. And prices are low. When I have a poor crop, so do my competitors, and prices are high. Year in and year out prices average out. Whether I stay in business or not depends on how efficiently I can produce apples.

On a cattle ranch in California our practice is to buy young cattle in the fall, put them on the range until June or July, when we sell. Here again prices vary from year to year, both the prices we pay and the prices we receive. They may be expected to average out.

In the long run, whether we make money or not depends on the feed conditions on the range and on our ability to put weight on at a low cost.

Next we come to dairying. In a previous lecture I referred to a dairy farm in San Mateo County, California. It is no country life plaything. We milk 500 cows a day. We are also in the retail business. Leave that out. It presents a marketing problem, under highly competitive conditions.

But in so far as production is concerned, the problem is this: I know just how much it costs to raise a cow, and how much to keep her during her productive years. I know what price I can expect to receive on the average for butterfat. If every cow in the barn cannot produce enough butterfat to pay for her keep and amortize her cost—or, in other words, if every cow is not an efficient productive unit—I lose money.

If I have not the ability to breed efficient producers, if I have not the judgment to cull inefficient producers, if I cannot keep my feed and other costs down, I cannot survive.

The lesson I have learned is that farming in one essential respect is no different from any other business. You either produce efficiently or you succumb to the pressure of competition.

A system of individual competition is not perfect. It has its casualties. But it does produce balance. It does contribute to a solution by correcting the causes.

The farm problem of the last few years would have been very different had this reality been firmly grasped; and were it not for the efforts to keep the inefficient producer on the land, and the inefficient land in production.

We have long looked upon the farm as more than a mere place to make a living. We think of the country as a desirable place to live. I am sufficiently old-fashioned to believe that the farm provides, in goodly measure, that discipline which goes far in moulding good citizens. The farm boy and girl are early placed upon their own. Day-to-day tasks present them with new situations. Duty requires them to be self-reliant. They must exercise initiative. Their environment, made up largely of growing, developing, and changing things, teaches them to think. Here one sees freedom of individual action at its best. It would be difficult, indeed, to designate a better school than the farm for citizenship in a democracy.

Certainly we will do well to pause before submerging that type of life in a system of centralized controls.

That this nation has been confronted with a serious agricultural situation, no one will deny.

The startling feature is that, while conditions in many respects have shown improvement, the complications are increasing.

Agriculturally speaking, the weather is foggy. Nations are doing queer things with, and to, agriculture.

England and Germany subsidize hog *production*. We subsidize hog *reduction*. In 1933 our government paid farmers to plow under 10,500,000 acres of cotton. Egypt, for example, accepted that opportunity by increasing her plantings 60 per cent over those of the previous year. In 1934, farmers were paid to keep 14,500,000 acres out of cotton. Brazil and other foreign cotton growing countries were not slow in filling this gap. Foreign cotton production has increased by amounts amazingly similar to our decreases.

In 1934, the United States subsidized wheat reduction by something like 7,800,000 acres. At the same time, Italy, a heavy consumer of imported wheat, was throwing the weight of government assistance behind the growing of more and more wheat.

Truly these are unusual times.

Over a century ago, Malthus won international recognition by expressing deep concern over the "pressure of the population upon the food supply." We have become highly excited over the pressure of the food supply upon the population. This excitement has led the government to assume extensive control over agriculture, and to inflict heavy burdens upon its consuming population. For the first time in the nation's history, the financial resources of government have been devoted to reducing the supply of the essentials of life.

In its zeal to reduce production, it has made non-compliance with its programs a criminal offense.

The results of government planning are in evidence. We spent huge sums to reduce supplies of wheat, cotton, corn, hogs, and tobacco. Nature stepped in uninvited, with a helping hand. Through the 1934 and 1936 droughts, she did some reducing on her own account. One result is an actual shortage of some of those things which were associated with what was termed, "burdening surpluses." Another result is the heavy importation of some of those very same commodities upon which much money and effort were expended in cutting down supplies. The country now finds itself in the embarrassing position of buying from others the things which our farmers produce most efficiently and most abundantly when unmolested with restrictive measures.

Government planning can never be applied to agriculture, except under a system of compulsion. Wheat reductions were not on a compulsory basis. Had there been no adverse court decision, the wheat program would have fallen of its own weight. The acreage sown to wheat, with the reduction program in force, in the fall of 1935 and the spring of 1936 was 5,000,000 acres, or eight per cent more than for the previous year. The 1936 acreage (still under the reduction program) was seven per cent in excess of the area planted, on the average, during the five-year period (1928–1932) immediately preceding the restriction program. The government paid vast sums for reducing wheat acreage. Yet had weather conditions been normal during the past year, we would have had greater production than before the program was undertaken. This means just one thing. Those not participating in the program increased their acreage more than participants reduced their sowings. In other words, increases in the less specialized wheat growing areas were greater than the reductions in the specialized wheat growing regions.

The intended results can be obtained only under a system of compulsory participation, covering all growers of the commodity in question.

But, in agriculture, even compulsion may not turn the trick. Nature is a most important controlling force. Nature does not submit to the strait-jacket of bureaucratic dictation.

Planning agricultural production gives rise to all of the general difficulties which we have noted elsewhere. In addition, it faces some peculiarly obstinate problems of its own.

To date, control has meant restriction of production upon efficient and inefficient alike.

With millions of families denied a liberal diet, it is hard to justify the deliberate curtailment of available food supplies.

And how it can be to the nation's advantage to forbid the efficient utilization of developed farms in admittedly good agricultural regions passes my comprehension. But, then, it is one of the vices of all these schemes based on monopolistic principles that they ignore efficiency, the rights of the efficient producer and the general welfare.

Looking at it from the farmers' standpoint, it is said that the small harvest brings more money than large crops. Even so, it does not follow that net farm incomes are enhanced by a scarcity program. Little to sell at a high price is a doubtful substitute for a less price for all that can be efficiently produced.

I am aware, as you are aware, of the excuse offered by those in authority for their unusual actions in placing a premium on not producing. They say that industry voluntarily restricted its activities and thereby "plowed men into the streets." The claim is that since industry curtails production and throttles agriculture's markets, agriculture must fight fire with fire, by diminishing its own output.

My answer is that national prosperity is not promoted by creating one destructive force to offset another destructive force. The welfare of the nation demands the elimination, not the multiplication, of such forces.

Thoughtful farmers will not be convinced that they should follow industry's example. When a manufacturer reduces production he also reduces his labor costs —a heavy cash item in most industries. Such is not the case with farmers. Their cash expenses are made up, in goodly part, of fixed costs such as taxes and interest. These go on just the same whether the farmer tills all or a part of his acres. Cutting down labor on most farms merely means less work for farmers and members of their families. Their cash expenses are not reduced by depriving themselves of work.

A program of growing less, with its resulting inefficiency in production, certainly does not solve the problem from the nation's point of view, and I seriously doubt if it results in anything more than passing benefits to agriculture.

There are a number of ways by which the government may improve the lot of farmers; ways which do not impair their individual initiative and freedom, or make them subjects of a dole in the guise of benefit payments, or reduce the national income.

The list of services rendered the farmer and safeguards given him by the Federal Government long before the New Deal was even a name is an impressive one. May I mention here a few of the more important agricultural measures enacted during the twelve-year period, 1920–1932:

I. *Cooperation.*

    (1) The Capper-Volstead Act for the first time gave recognition to the farmers' cooperative movement.

    (2) The Division of Cooperative Marketing was created in 1926. It continues to function today as a research and service agency.

    (3) Whatever may have been the shortcomings of the stabilization operations, the Farm Board, created in 1929, rendered substantial services to cooperative marketing. The Bank for Cooperatives in the Farm Credit Administration is an outgrowth of the activities of the Farm Board.

    (4) In 1927, Boards of Trade and Produce Exchanges were compelled to admit farmers' cooperative organizations to membership.

II. *Aid to Livestock Producers.*

    In 1921, the Packers' and Stockyards' Act placed the operation of packing plants and stockyards under government supervision.

III. *Commodity Exchanges.*

>In 1922, the Grain Futures Act provided for government regulation and supervision of grain exchanges.

IV. *Fruits and Vegetables.*

>In the interest of "fair practice," definite standards for fruit and vegetable containers were fixed; the Perishable Agricultural Commodity Act suppressed unfair and fraudulent practices in interstate commerce; canned goods were brought under the pure food and drug act; the inspection service and market news service were greatly extended.

V. *Agricultural Credit.*

>Intermediate Credit Banks were established; new laws were passed making provision for crop and production loans; the Reconstruction Finance Corporation was established.

In addition, large sums were appropriated for the prevention of diseases of plants and animals, and the eradication of insect pests. Battles against the foot-and-mouth disease, the European corn-borer, and the Mediterranean fruit-fly-are-outstanding examples.

The interests of the farmer were evidently not entirely neglected even before the dawn of the managed millennium.

Much of what has been done under the New Deal is praiseworthy and helpful. The supply of ample farm credit for long and short terms, the prompt relief from drought, flood and similar disasters, the soil conservation program,—are all examples in principle of sound measures for assistance to agriculture.

I say "in principle," because I cannot approve all of the details of the measures themselves, or of the manner in which they were administered.

Take soil conservation, for example.

Soil conservation is a national problem. It is of universal import. The city dweller, as well as the farmer, is interested in defending our national resources against waste and depletion. The soil is one of the most important of these. The dust bowls of the West, flood devastations of the East, ever encroaching gullies of the South, together with the loss of fertility over wide areas, are conspicuous reminders of the pressing need for corrective action.

This is a problem that will always be with us. It demands constant watchfulness. There is no controversy as to the desirability of government participation in this field. The question that I raise is that of merging a long-time national, universally accepted program with measures having to do with temporary farm relief expediencies. I do not believe it wise to use the light truck of conservation to haul the heavy trailer of farm relief. Each should be independent of the other. Their destinations are not the same. If conservation is to live as a continuing policy, its payments must be on a basis that can be justified after the need for farm relief has passed.

There are other ways of strengthening farm life.

There is a wise land use program. We now have farms where no farms should be. Land has been plowed that should never have been plowed. A lack of a national land policy has contributed to an impoverished agriculture. The correction of this situation is a legitimate government function. It calls for government acquisition or control of abandoned and non-productive farm land.

Instead of a blanket program carried out according to dictates from Washington, it should be made sufficiently flexible to fit local conditions and to supplement state and local plans of zoning, land purchase, or reforestation. We must not permit the weight of Federal funds to continue to dictate policy, and to dominate action in matters of so vital concern to state and local communities.

Tenancy is a matter of growing concern. Today 42 out of every 100 farms are operated by renters. In some regions the percentage is considerably higher. This is not a desirable state of affairs. I consider it an accepted function of government to encourage farm ownership. In doing this, extreme care should be exercised to the end that government action be on a self-liquidating basis. Otherwise, the farm is likely to become a dumping ground for those attracted by bounties, rather than by the desire or ability to farm.

In planning to reduce tenancy, care should be exercised to the end that the prospective owner does not become a ward of the government. The tenant-recipient of government funds must not be reduced to the status of an Indian on a reservation.

All will agree that the American farmer should be given preference in the domestic market for those products he can produce efficiently. Efficient production includes most of our farm staples.

But American agriculture is also vitally dependent on sales abroad. In 1929, we exported 55 per cent of our cotton; 41 per cent of our leaf tobacco; 33 per cent of our lard; 18 per cent of our wheat; 15 per cent of our apples; 46 per cent of our dried fruits; and 23 per cent of our canned fruits.

On an average, during the twenties, it required from 60,000,000 to 70,000,000 acres to supply foreign demand. In 1935, this figure dropped to 27,000,000.

What is even more discouraging—while our export trade has been improving since the bottom of the depression was reached in 1932, recovery has been entirely confined to non-agricultural products.

The quantity of non-agricultural exports in 1936 stood at 67 per cent of the 1929 level.

The 1936 volume of farm exports amounted to only 43 per cent of the pre-depression peak, and was the smallest since 1877.

This situation is due in part to the desire for self-sufficiency, in part to the inability of nations to import because they cannot export. Italy, for example, has placed a prohibitive tariff on wheat. She grows her own without regard to cost. One reason for this is her inability to sell her products in foreign markets. Germany will not take those things we grow cheaply and abundantly—wheat and lard—because we do not buy what she produces cheaply and abundantly.

Expansion of export outlets, above their present levels, offers rich potential opportunities. On behalf of agriculture, every legitimate effort should be exercised by our government to promote the export of American agricultural products through the resumption of foreign trade.

All of these policies, every one of them within the

Constitutional powers of the Federal Government, would be greatly beneficial to agriculture.

But if the American farmer is to proceed on his own, uncontrolled and unhampered, he must, above all, be assured of equality of opportunity.

(a) He must not be subject to tariff inequality.

(b) He must not pay tribute to monopoly.

(c) He must not suffer from his inability to organize for his own protection as efficiently as can other groups.

Let us look at each of these in turn:

Tariff Inequality.

Now, what is the situation with respect to some of our major crops of which there is a substantial exportable surplus? The surplus is sold in world markets, and the price of the entire crop is determined by world prices. Tariff protection on these crops, generally speaking, is ineffective. These farmers sell in a free market and buy many of their needs in a protected market. This situation has existed for many years. But until fairly recently the surplus was readily absorbed abroad at acceptable prices. At the same time, our unusually high standard of living furnished the farmer with an ever-expanding and highly prosperous home market for his products.

It is probably true that so long as these conditions prevailed, the theoretical handicap under which the farmer labored was pretty much offset. In any event, prior to the Great War, the farmer shared increasingly in America's prosperity. Conditions today are entirely different. World markets are largely closed to our agricultural surpluses.

We hope and pray that the world will come to its senses. We are justified in going to great lengths to promote the resumption of normal foreign trade. The farmer stands to benefit most from this action.

The question is, what are we to do for the farmer in the meantime?

In the national interest, we do not want the efficient farmer to be forced off a good farm.

Even if he did move, he could not move rapidly and in any great numbers and be absorbed by our urban groups.

Two courses seem open and they both offer real difficulties:

We can lower tariff rates on those things which figure prominently in farm consumption.

Or temporarily until world markets are reopened we can give him a compensatory cash bounty.

I must add, however, that of the many bounty plans suggested I have not seen one that appeared to me remotely satisfactory. In principle, however, such bounties are justifiable.

Curbing of Monopoly Power.

In proposing measures for protecting the farmer against exactions by monopoly, I can do no better than quote from the Republican Platform of 1936:

A private monopoly is indefensible and intolerable. It menaces and, if continued, will utterly destroy constitutional government and the liberty of the citizen.

We favor the vigorous enforcement of the criminal laws, as well as the civil laws, against monopolies and trusts and their officials, and we demand the enactment of such additional legislation as is necessary to make it impossible for private monopoly to exist in the United States.

We will employ the full powers of the Government to the end that monopoly shall be eliminated and that free enterprise shall be fully restored and maintained.

Farm Impacts of Organized Labor.

Of course, if the government under some plan such as N.R.A. forces up the price of all that the farmer buys, we cannot quarrel with government organization of the farmers to force up the price of agricultural products.

But, let us not ignore that these two joint and complementary efforts, by raising prices, reducing consumption and curtailing the production of wealth, would inevitably result in national impoverishment.

By this time you know how whole-heartedly I condemn any such program.

But certainly in a free society labor can organize for its own protection. No sensible person would in any way restrict its right to do so. Having organized, it may bargain to its own advantage.

The farmer, because of the nature of his business, is unable to organize efficiently for purposes of price control. He has here a real cause for anxiety in case other groups exercise this power.

Let me illustrate.

The U. S. Steel Corporation recently increased its annual wage bill by $130,000,000 under threat of a strike. The increased price schedule immediately put into effect passed the cost on to the consumers of steel.

The farmer has a right to worry. But in this respect

he is no differently situated than all other consumers.

If wage increases are simply to result in price increases, then we are in for trouble. As we have seen, the basis of our steady progress is due to our ability so to increase our productive efficiency as to make more and more goods available to more and more people at lower and lower prices. This has been the one immense contribution of mass production to human welfare. And as we have likewise seen, labor has steadily benefited through shorter hours and higher real wages. But these benefits to labor have been the fruits of increased efficiency—not of higher prices.

It may be that wage earners are entitled to higher money wages. As to that I express no opinion.

But this is certain. Unless the higher money wages can be absorbed by industry, and not passed on to the consumer in the form of higher prices, it means the arresting of progress.

Higher prices—I am not talking of a general rise in the price level, but of individual increases caused artificially—mean lower consumption, because fewer and fewer people can buy. Less consumption means less production—that is, fewer and fewer goods to divide.

This is not a farm problem. It is a national problem. For if carried far enough it must result in a lower standard of living for all, and more particularly for the lowest income group.

The good sense of American labor can be relied on to see this as clearly as we do.

If, however, the farmer is not satisfied to rely on the common sense of his fellow workers, but invokes the power of government to balance the scale, does he not incur an even greater risk?

Government power means political power. And political power gravitates in the direction of the most votes. If production and prices are to be controlled by government, the farmer in the long run will get the worst of it, for the balance of political power lies very definitely with the city dweller.

In conclusion, may I restate my agricultural thesis simply and briefly.

Agriculture is a group of industries. Its problems are many and varied. Government intervention on behalf of one set of producers may easily cause hardships to another set. This situation throws a responsibility upon the individual farmer, which he cannot well evade. It is my belief that he does not choose to evade it. His interests and the interests of the nation demand that he be granted the utmost freedom of economic action within his own line fence. Outside that fence, he has the right to insist that he be accorded that equality of opportunity enjoyed by other business and labor groups. He must not be the victim of tariff burdens. He rightfully demands that he not pay tribute to monopoly. And he may respectfully request that organized labor not inflict upon him increased prices. It is government's sphere to see to it that the farmer is not the victim of other pressure groups. This duty performed, the farmer is then in position to go ahead in his own way, under his own power—unhampered and uncontrolled.

It is to the nation's advantage that he be permitted to do so.

CHAPTER VIII

LABOR

HERE, where almost everyone works, where there are no fixed classes, where the door is wide open to the industrious and able, and where today's captain of industry is yesterday's wage earner, the term "labor" includes us all.

Assuredly it does in this sense: that all those productively engaged, whether on the farm, in the shop, in the store, in the mine, in giving service, in the manager's office or in individual enterprise, are united by ties of mutual interests and by a common purpose.

That purpose is so to increase productivity as to raise the standard of living of all; and no group can selfishly seek its own welfare at the expense of other groups without betraying this common cause.

If employers, having suppressed competition, charge unconscionable prices for their goods, or sweat their workers, lower consumption and decreased purchasing power will be followed by reduced production.

If farmers, aided by government, cut necessary production and unduly raise prices, they may temporarily profit—but all other groups suffer, and the nation is the poorer.

If wage earners use their right of association to compel a reduction in hours or increase in money wages that cannot be offset by increased efficiency and must be passed on in higher prices, it can only mean that there will be fewer goods to divide.

The American nation is not made up of mutually antagonistic groups. Rather is it composed of an infinite number of partnerships, that in turn form one great partnership. The partners may differ at times as to their relative rewards, but, fundamentally, their interests are the same.

There has never been a place in American life for class warfare.

Ours is a classless society. Our industrial, financial and political leaders for the most part come from the ranks. They were once wage earners. In spite of differences of wealth and achievement, one man is considered as good as another. Immediate interests may differ, but there is a common point of view. In the past, mutual understanding and cooperation have prevailed. They account in no small measure for our success in raising the standard of living of the American wage earner to a record level.

Mutuality of interests, understanding and cooperation,—these are the true foundations of general prosperity.

The second point I want to emphasize is that labor problems are primarily local problems. They fall within the jurisdiction of the States rather than of the Federal Government.

Both as regards living and working conditions, the lives of the millions gainfully employed are governed by their immediate environment. Conditions differ greatly—in country and city, in village and town, and even in the great cities. Prices, rents, costs of living, standards and modes of life vary from region to region and from community to community.

There is an immense volume of business that begins and terminates within a very limited area, and in which labor questions cannot be other than local. And even in the case of great corporations, with factories and establishments in several States and a national market, wages, hours of work and working conditions are not uniform in the several establishments.

The States are much better fitted to deal with labor problems sympathetically and understandingly in the light of their more intimate knowledge of local factors. It is for this reason that we hold the States responsible, for instance, for housing conditions and slum clearances; for the health, safety and welfare of workers; and for such measures as compensation, child labor and maximum hours and minimum wage laws.

So, too, in the matter of relationship between employers and employees and of their respective rights—a question that recently has been forcibly brought to public attention—the States are the proper administrative and policy determining bodies. They are much closer to the picture. Administratively, they can act with greater knowledge, promptness and effectiveness. When it comes to legislation, they are more responsive to the temper and will of their people than Washington can be. And labor problems in different sections of the country vary widely, as do many other problems. Uniformity is undesirable and difficult of attainment.

The Wagner Labor Relations Act is defective in

several important particulars. It imposes an impossible task on the Board in determining when there has been a failure to bargain collectively. It confers important rights on unions but imposes no obligations and responsibilities. Unless restricted to cases directly affecting interstate commerce in an important way, it may mean the assumption by the Federal Government of complete jurisdiction over employer-employee relationships throughout the United States. From an administrative standpoint, such thorough-going centralization is unsound. If every dispute, however trivial, is brought to Washington, the Board will be swamped —or compelled to create a far-flung and immense bureaucratic organization. From a practical standpoint, a Central Board, lacking local background, is nothing like as effective in adjusting differences as a local one.

It is interesting that when the test came in the Michigan strikes, the Wagner Act was ignored by all concerned. The strikes were looked upon as Michigan's problems, to be dealt with in Michigan, by Michigan authorities. No other course would have served as well. The President himself would not have been as useful a mediator as Governor Murphy. He is not a Michigan man; and the people in Michigan knew that this was Michigan's business.

Our States have their roots in deep.

Anyone who believes, as I do, in the freedom of the individual must insist on the right of employees to organize—a right which carries with it the privilege of selecting their own representatives in their dealings with employers.

In the exercise of this right they are entitled to the protection of the law—that is, employers should be forbidden to bring pressure to bear on employees to prevent their joining the union of their choice.

But those who believe in freedom likewise hold that the individual working man has an equally valid right not to join a union. This right too must be respected— that is, the union must be forbidden to coerce or intimidate him into joining, either in his home or in his place of work. Compulsory membership through any such system as the check-off should not be countenanced.

If membership in unions—the right to organize, to bargain and to select representatives being fully protected by law—were on a strictly voluntary basis, free from any taint of coercion, unions would gain immeasurably in standing and influence. The suspicion that men have been forced to join against their will and that the union is not, therefore, truly representative, would disappear. Under these conditions the very fact of its existence would be proof of its value to those it serves, and of its right to speak for them.

That a union should not assume to speak for those who are not its members would seem to be common sense and common fairness.

If the majority of wage earners in a plant are union members, it is true that, as a practical matter, the terms of their agreement with the employer will govern working conditions. That is as it should be, but this does not mean that the minority should be denied the right of organization or the right to be heard.

Here again the Wagner Act is open to criticism. The

argument that all it does is to apply democratic principles to this particular situation does not hold water. If the terms of the Wagner law were applied in the political sphere, it would mean that, the Democrats having received a majority of the votes last Fall, the seventeen million Republicans could have no representation in Congress, must disband their party organization, and, to have any voice or influence, must collectively and individually join the New Deal Party.

There is a Hitlerian touch to this conception of democracy.

The strike is a legitimate and labor's most powerful weapon. In the collectivist states, such as Germany, Italy and, of course, Russia, strikes are forbidden. That would not do in a free society where the thought of compulsory labor under conditions fixed by government edict is abhorrent.

But even the most legitimate of weapons can be abused to the point of illegality. There have been altogether too much violence, lawlessness and intimidation connected with strikes in this country. Both sides have offended. Violence and lawlessness raise a strong presumption against the justice of a cause. They antagonize public sentiment. They disgust reasonable men.

The sit-down strike is an outstanding example of this sort of abuse.

It begins by defying the law and ends by defying the government.

It strikes at the very foundations of society. A free society exists only by virtue of a common agreement to conform to accepted standards of conduct; to abide by the decision of the majority as expressed in the law;

and to recognize the authority of those chosen by the people to give effect to their will.

No civilized society can exist without order, and there can be no order where there is no respect for law. If the members of a free society transgress the rules they themselves have established, or violate the conditions essential to its continued existence, the alternative is the strong arm of despotic authority. For men and women cannot live in a state of anarchy and chaos, and rather than perish they will abandon freedom, and look to autocratic power for salvation.

I am not seriously concerned. I believe that we have witnessed a passing phase. American labor has too much sense to pursue such an issue to the end. American labor does not want either to challenge or to destroy the authority of government.

It has before it the fate of labor unions in Italy and Germany. They started out, flushed with power, to dominate the State. They ended by being its slaves.

But if the unions cannot bring themselves to live within the law, then the States would do well to turn for guidance—to Great Britain—the mother of trade unionism—and to consider legislation along the lines of the British Trades Disputes Act of 1927, modified to meet local conditions.

Under the Act,—

Unions cannot strike against the State.

Forms of sympathetic strikes for ulterior motives are outlawed.

Intimidation and coercion, either in connection with organizing campaigns or picketing, are unequivocally illegal.

Privileges and immunities, such as protection of union funds, are guaranteed only if unions report their income and expenditures in detail to a public official.

Contributions to political funds cannot be made obligatory upon members and cannot be drawn from the general funds of the union.

I am against compulsory arbitration. In effect it deprives labor of the right to strike. It vests in government the final decision as to wages and working conditions. It is only a short step from there to government control, and to all those rigidities that are fatal to progress.

But a well established and thorough system of mediation would be beneficial.

Looking to the future, success or failure of trade unionism will depend upon the one test that counts: what benefits unionism brings to labor. The ultimate decision rests with the wage earner. He still has freedom of choice, and he will make the decision, as a practical man, in the light of benefits received.

High wages and good working conditions are the result of prosperity. Prosperity depends upon efficient production that turns out a good article at a low cost. It depends upon a willingness to forego immediate for long-time benefits; upon good management enjoying a wide measure of freedom; upon a harmonious, contented and cooperative organization; and, last but not least, upon flexibility and adaptiveness to changing conditions.

The achievements of the motor industry are a good example of the kind of prosperity that brings real benefits to labor.

The story of the Ford Company, as told by William J. Cameron in one of the Ford evening hours, is illustrative of the process of growth and its consequent rewards. Someone had written Cameron asking the question:

If all Ford profits had been given to the help, how much additional would they have received? * * *

Mr. Cameron answers the question as follows:

Taking the inquiry literally, as asking how much more Ford employes would have received had all the profits been divided among them, the answer is that there would be no Ford employes, no Ford profits, no Ford Motor Company, and no one concerned with this question and answer tonight. Let us see why. * * *

Henry Ford began business in a little shop with seventy-five men. * * * Anyone can see what would have happened had he called his men together every week and divided among them the week's profit. What would have been left for experiment, equipment, improvement, growth? Nothing. * * *

The little shop would have stayed little. Its crude methods would have remained crude. Its primitive car would not have advanced beyond the primitive stage. * * * The little Ford shop, dispersing its profits, would have drifted farther and farther behind, grown more and more antiquated, until eventually it disappeared, and seventy-five men would have been out. * * *

For if profits had not been continuously fed back into the business there would have been no business, and consequently no employes.

But, conserved and invested in the business, these profits did much more for the employes than tonight's question suggests.

They produced in wages four times as much as all the profits amounted to; they supplied the nation with 25,000,-000 useful vehicles; they increased those original seventy-five Ford jobs to 125,000 Ford jobs, and made possible 200,-000 other jobs in outside industries and they supported government with $600,000,000 in taxes. * * *

Continuing, Mr. Cameron pointed out that what the question really referred to was not profits but dividends, and that had dividends of the last ten years been added to wages, it would have meant for each man a wage increase of only about 3 cents an hour.

Says Mr. Cameron:

These amounts are not very exciting when we consider that the actual increase in Ford wages during thirty-three years was about 400%.

He concludes,

the philosophy of taking everything, whether practiced by management or labor, or by both together, or by government tax collectors, results in nobody's getting anything. * * *

Though little affected either by unionism or legislation, real wages have steadily risen over a long period of time, and working conditions have improved. In the period of the 1920's, when trade unionism was at its lowest ebb, including less than 10% of the wage-earning lower-salaried population, unexampled strides in real wages were made.

In 25 manufacturing industries real wages increased on the average by 14½ per cent. from 1920 to 1929; in the automobile industry they increased by over 18 per cent.; in foundries and machine shops, by over 12; in the chemical industry, by over 22 per cent.; in the paper and pulp industry, by over 8 per cent.; in the printing book and job industry, by over 32 per cent.; while the real wages of yard engineers in Class I railroads increased by over 19 per cent.

We do have unscrupulous employers. They do take advantage of economic pressure on individuals. But they are not representative of American employers as a class.

Individual employers in the United States have made notable advances—voluntarily—in labor relations. They have granted great benefits to their employees, such as group life insurance, health and sickness benefits, vacations with pay, thrift funds—benefits rarely found under union arrangements.

Without wise leadership there is danger that by their inflexibility, unions may act as a brake on prosperity and expansion. Their constant pressure for shorter hours, regardless of whether conditions justify them, as exemplified today by the demand for a thirty-hour week; their willingness to force up costs, even at the expense of stagnation and unemployment, as witness the building trades; the needs of their leaders, periodically, to fortify their authority by devising new demands; the limitations imposed upon plant management; and the element of rigidity which they inject into an organization, may not be ineradicable weaknesses, but they cannot be ignored.

Rigidities are particularly serious in periods of business recession, when prices must come down to meet a diminishing demand. Wages should not drop as fast, or as far, as prices. But there must be some give. If, because of rigid costs, prices cannot be adjusted to demand, goods will not move, production slackens, and the unemployment which follows contributes to the downward movement.

Unionization, no matter how powerful, can by itself contribute little to improve the condition of the worker or to prevent a decline in his standard of living during a depression. It is a matter of general knowledge that during the recent depression the workers in such well-organized industries in this country as coal, railroads, clothing, and building have been no more successful in escaping unemployment and reduction in earnings than those in the unorganized trades. As a matter of fact, the building and coal industries have suffered most. I do not say that they would have fared better if the workers had not been organized, but only that economic forces much stronger than unionization determine the ability of an industry to support the people attached to it.

International comparisons lead to the same conclusion. In England, organized labor has been an economic and political power for many years, and England has pioneered in labor legislation. The fact that labor in the United States has obtained, without the help of labor unionism, a higher standard of living than the English worker, requires little statistical proof. During most of the post-war period England has been in a state of depression. Only recently there appeared signs of a general recovery—a recovery with which labor unions certainly had nothing to do. From

1920 to 1929, British labor unions were unable to prevent a drastic decline in weekly wages. In eight representative British industries the decline in weekly wages
during the period varied from 13.8 per cent. to 42.8 per
cent. The largest decline occurred in the shipbuilding
industry, which was one of the most depressed; and
the lowest in the boot and shoe industry, which produces consumers' goods and is, therefore, relatively
more stable.

Organized labor in Germany was successful in increasing wage rates after the stabilization of the German mark at the end of 1923. From 1924 to 1929 the
increase in real wages amounted to almost 50 per cent.;
money wages during the same period rose 80 per cent.
This accomplishment was due almost entirely to the
political power of organized labor during the life of
the German Republic. But history would have perhaps
dealt less severely with the German labor unions if
they had been less successful in compelling the employers to grant wage increases. Money wages rose
twice as rapidly as the physical volume of production,
and most of the benefits obtained by industry through
rationalization or improvements in technique were absorbed by labor in increased wages. An unsound economic and political situation was created before the
depression. It was made more difficult after the out-
break of the depression, owing to the refusal of the
trade unions to accept wage reductions. The German
wage structure collapsed only in 1932 after the virtual
collapse of German democracy.

It is extremely difficult to make international wage
comparisons because of differences in standards of liv-

ing. Figures of the International Labor Office, however, show that from 1913 to 1927 real wages rose 30 per cent. in the United States; 27 per cent. in Sweden; 5 per cent. in Great Britain; and that they declined 5 per cent. in France and 2 per cent. in Germany. Obviously, the ability of a country or of an industry to provide the workers with a high standard of living is determined by fundamental economic forces and not by the power of labor unionism.

I state these facts in no spirit of antagonism or criticism. But because they must be faced if labor unionism is to grow, to be a strong and healthy element in our national life, and to make the contribution it can to the welfare and prosperity of its members and of the country.

As I view it, unions can be strong, healthy and helpful only if they are built up on a voluntary basis, deriving their strength—as does every other lasting instrumentality of progress—from demonstrated value and usefulness.

I emphasize the word "voluntary," because there is another method of growth—through the direct exercise of political power. That is, the authority of government may be invoked in effect to compel all wage earners to join unions, irrespective of economic benefits. And the then enormously expanded political strength may next be used completely to dominate or even control the government in the interests of a class.

Such a program might temporarily triumph. But control of government by a dominant minority would destroy the foundation of democratic institutions. It would threaten the rights and welfare of the majority.

It would provoke a violent reaction. The majority would assert itself. The minority would be brought under control. This might be accomplished without damage to our institutions and to the cause of trade unionism—but there's a dreadful risk.

We cannot study recent history in Italy and Germany without realizing the danger.

Let me give you a recently published summary of events in the two countries:

ITALY

Scene 1

Post-war Italy, torn by internal strife, close to economic collapse, a weak government unable to make headway against the deadening aftermath of war. Labor, the best organized of struggling factions, determined to secure economic power for itself. Extensive demands made by the Federation of Metal Workers are flatly refused by employers. Labor, spurning so weak a weapon as a strike, occupies factories and even attempts to operate them. The government urges employers to grant concessions, but they refuse to negotiate until their factories are vacated. Workers respond by adding to their demands insistence on a permanent share in the control of industry.

The government declares neutrality. It will not eject those illegally occupying factories because it will not risk the danger of bloodshed. Finally, it intervenes on the side of labor and insists on concessions from employers, including the cession to workers of a share in the technical and financial control of industrial establishments. Organized labor has established its power—for the moment.

Scene 2

Industrial chaos has been succeeded by industrial reconstruction under the firm discipline of Mussolini. From the struggles of discordant groups rises the Fascist State, brooking no interference with progress toward its destiny. Even labor, recently so powerful, must accept and play the role allotted to it. * * * * *

That there may be no doubt about the status of labor in the Fascist State, Mussolini promulgates the Labor Charter (1927). Labor is under the protection of the State and is directed and controlled by the State. Collective bargaining through trade associations and trade unions is provided for. The State may revoke the right of collective bargaining at will, nor need it justify such action. Trade disputes concern the State more intimately than the parties to the dispute. The State, therefore, provides Labor Courts whose competence is universal and against whose decisions there is no appeal. Suspension of work by means of strikes or lockouts is a crime in the nature of sedition.

None of labor's bitter protests avail. Its demonstration of power has won for it only control by the State.

****

GERMANY

Scene 1

Industrial Germany re-establishing itself after the collapse of 1918 and the period of acute inflation that followed. The Socialist parties, embracing the working population and dominated by the trade unions, struggle against the employers and capitalists for control of the government. Socialist coalition governments abet unions in establishing their policies. One of the strongest trade union movements in the world is developed. Wage agreements are negotiated between unions and employers' association, legally binding, and at their expiration they cannot be revised downward. Federal government may intervene in labor disputes and require arbitration by appointees of a politically-controlled Minister of Labor. This official may, at his discretion, make awards binding. If employers refuse to abide by awards, their property may be seized.

Since the Socialists control the government and union labor controls the Socialists, government partiality toward the labor cause is inevitable. As a result, labor never loses under arbitration and wages are forced steadily upward without regard to economic justification. Employers are legally compelled to recognize unions, although unions represent a minority of all workers. Thus, unions are permitted to negotiate on behalf of all workers. * * * * *

Scene 2

Hitler, the era of National Socialism, the subordination of all interests to the will of The Leader, and the promotion of National Socialist principles. Class warfare is banned as wasteful, an impediment to national progress. Labor unions, as such, and employers' associations are abolished and strikes are forbidden. Employers and employees are organized in the Labor Front, rigidly controlled by the government. Group negotiation is replaced by individual dealings.

The employer is "the leader" of the establishment, the employees are his followers. The leader shall make all decisions for his followers. He is aided by a Confidential Council of representatives of employees who advise him with respect to all measures for strengthening mutual confidence and improving conditions of operation. To offset the great power given to the employer, labor trustees are appointed to represent the State. A majority of a confidential council may, on behalf of the employees, appeal decisions of the leader to the trustee. The labor trustee oversees the fulfillment of the general labor policy of the government, maintains industrial peace, and decides disputes between the leader and council of an establishment in his district. His decision is final because he represents the State, which is the supreme authority. The leader and labor trustee derive their power from the State and exercise their authority because no group or interest may challenge the State. Labor may be organized, but for State, not class, benefit.*

* National Industrial Conference Board—A Pageant of Labor Progress.

Labor organizations have a great opportunity to perform a genuine public service in protecting the rights and promoting the welfare of the wage earner, and in contributing to national prosperity. But they must eradicate the weaknesses and defects that in the past have frequently militated against their usefulness and strength:

They should:

1. Recognize the solidarity of interests between all classes, employers and employees included; and that the prosperity of the wage earner depends upon the prosperity of the industry.

2. Emphasize cooperation, mutual understanding and agreement, rather than the selfish application of power—and here employers must meet them more than half-way.

3. Refrain from coercion, intimidation and all forms of lawlessness.

4. Establish beyond question the voluntary character of their membership.

5. Realize the necessity of flexibility and adaptiveness to changing conditions and the dangers of artificial rigidities.

6. Make adequate financial reports to their members.

7. Accept legal responsibility as entities for their acts.

8. Avoid improper pressure on government—as exemplified by Mr. Lewis' call on President Roosevelt to support him in his sit-down strikes because of financial and other support in the past campaign.

This last does not mean that labor has not the right openly to advocate such measures as it deems wise before our State and Federal Governments.

It does not mean that labor leaders cannot support in elections the candidates of their choice—though it would be unfortunate from the public standpoint and of their own interests for labor, contrary to American tradition, to vote on class lines.

It does not mean that there should not be a labor party, though this would call for subjection to all laws and regulations other parties are subject to; a strict differentiation between political and economic activities; and the segregation of political funds from the funds of the union.

I doubt the success in this country of any party organized on a strictly class basis; and I am sure that such a course would militate against labor union usefulness and strength in other directions. As to this, opinions will differ.

To put it all in a few words, the philosophy that runs throughout these lectures applies to the problems of wage earners and their organizations just as it governs all other elements in a free society.

As a class, wage earners and their organizations must neither control nor be controlled by government. They have certain unalienable rights, and in the enjoyment of those rights they are entitled to the full protection of the law. Conversely, they are expected to respect the rights of others.

But, once secure from discrimination, coercion and any other unfair practices, labor organizations must be prepared to stand on their own feet; and to succeed or fail according to their demonstrated value and usefulness in contributing to the well-being of their members and to the material, moral and spiritual progress of the nation.

CONCLUSION

THE menace of collectivism casts an ever-lengthening shadow over American life. One by one the safeguards that protect the individual and his freedom are being undermined or destroyed. In sharp contrast with those who created this nation, today millions of sincere men and women either rank so-called security above freedom, or comfort themselves with the illusory belief that the individual can transfer his burdens and problems to government without sacrificing his liberties.

They will find to their sorrow that the collectivist road leads neither to security, nor to peace, nor to progress—but to tyranny, poverty and war.

The thesis of this book is that the aspirations of the people can be realized within the framework of our institutions; that the principles these institutions embody are as valid today as when first proclaimed; and that our written Constitution, our Federal form of government and our system of checks and balances are sufficiently flexible to meet new conditions and new needs. That they are as essential as ever to secure the blessings of liberty is not open to question. We have but to look at world events to realize as never before the transcendent value of the Bill of Rights, of independent tribunals, of democracy in government, and of all the safeguards that protect free men and free institutions.

But the mere preservation of forms and structure—important as it is—does not suffice. The fate of nations is determined more by the character of the people than by the character of government. In fact, in the long run, the character of the government is determined by the character of the people.

If the promise of American life, as we have hitherto understood it, is to be realized, there must be a revival of faith—faith in our institutions, faith in our future, faith in each other, and faith in ourselves. There must be an end to this everlasting looking to government for guidance and support. There must be a return to those most characteristic of American virtues: confidence, enterprise, industry, courage—and, above all, self-reliance.

Two courses still remain open to us. We can individually and collectively continue to be responsible for our own destiny; and, as free men, look upon government as a servant, not a master. Or we can put government in the driver's seat and become mere passengers, looking for a safe, perhaps a free, ride.

But, in making this choice, let us at least face the incontrovertible fact that if we grant government sufficient power to master our destiny, we grant it sufficient power to master us.

Reduced to its simplest terms, this is the issue that confronts the American people.